50 Cheese Lover's Guide Recipes for Home

By: Kelly Johnson

Table of Contents

- Classic Mac and Cheese
- Four-Cheese Lasagna
- Cheese-Stuffed Meatballs
- Cheese Fondue
- Cheddar Cheese Soup
- Cheese-Stuffed Pretzels
- Grilled Cheese Sandwich
- Caprese Salad with Fresh Mozzarella
- Baked Brie with Honey and Nuts
- Cheese and Bacon Stuffed Mushrooms
- Pimento Cheese Spread
- Cheese Quesadillas
- Blue Cheese and Walnut Salad
- Cheesy Scalloped Potatoes
- Cheese-Stuffed Chicken Breast
- Spinach and Cheese Stuffed Manicotti
- Cheese Soufflé
- Cheeseburger Sliders
- Cheese Pizza
- Ricotta Cheese Pancakes
- Cheese-Stuffed Jalapeños
- Feta and Spinach Stuffed Phyllo Pastries
- Cheese and Broccoli Casserole
- Cheese and Herb Focaccia
- Cheese Enchiladas
- Gouda and Apple Grilled Cheese
- Cheese-Stuffed Burger
- Cheese and Tomato Tart
- Parmesan-Crusted Chicken
- Cheese-Stuffed Peppers
- Three-Cheese Omelet
- Cheesy Garlic Bread
- Cheese and Herb Scones
- Cheese and Spinach Quiche
- Cheesy Grits

- Cheese and Sausage Breakfast Casserole
- Cheese Ravioli
- Mozzarella Sticks
- Cheese-Stuffed Meatloaf
- Cheese and Herb Biscuits
- Cheese-Topped French Onion Soup
- Cheese-Stuffed Zucchini Boats
- Cheese and Apple Platter
- Cheesy Cauliflower Bake
- Cheese-Stuffed Soft Pretzels
- Cheesy Nachos
- Cheese and Broccoli Soup
- Cheese and Chive Scones
- Cheese and Bacon Dip
- Cheese-Stuffed Chicken Parmesan

Four-Cheese Lasagna

Ingredients:

- 12 lasagna noodles
- 2 cups ricotta cheese
- 2 cups shredded mozzarella cheese
- 1 cup grated Parmesan cheese
- 1 cup crumbled gorgonzola cheese
- 2 cups marinara sauce
- 1 egg
- 2 cloves garlic, minced
- 1 tablespoon dried basil
- 1 tablespoon dried oregano
- Salt and pepper to taste
- Fresh parsley, chopped (optional, for garnish)

Instructions:

1. Preheat Oven: Preheat your oven to 375°F (190°C).
2. Cook Noodles: Cook the lasagna noodles according to the package instructions until al dente. Drain and set aside.
3. Prepare Cheese Mixture: In a large bowl, combine ricotta cheese, 1 1/2 cups of mozzarella cheese, 1/2 cup of Parmesan cheese, gorgonzola cheese, egg, minced garlic, dried basil, dried oregano, salt, and pepper. Mix until well combined.
4. Layer Lasagna:
    - Spread a thin layer of marinara sauce at the bottom of a 9x13 inch baking dish.
    - Place a layer of lasagna noodles on top of the sauce.
    - Spread a layer of the cheese mixture over the noodles.
    - Repeat the layers: marinara sauce, noodles, and cheese mixture until you reach the top of the baking dish. The top layer should be noodles.
5. Top with Cheese:
    - Spread the remaining marinara sauce over the top layer of noodles.
    - Sprinkle the remaining mozzarella and Parmesan cheese evenly over the top.
6. Bake: Cover the baking dish with aluminum foil and bake in the preheated oven for 25 minutes. Then, remove the foil and bake for an additional 20-25 minutes, or until the cheese on top is melted and bubbly and the lasagna is heated through.
7. Cool and Serve: Let the lasagna cool for about 10 minutes before slicing. Garnish with fresh parsley, if desired, and serve hot.

Enjoy your delicious, cheesy Four-Cheese Lasagna!

Cheese-Stuffed Meatballs

Ingredients:

- 1 lb ground beef
- 1 lb ground pork
- 1 cup breadcrumbs
- 1/2 cup grated Parmesan cheese
- 2 cloves garlic, minced
- 1 small onion, finely chopped
- 1/4 cup chopped fresh parsley
- 1 egg
- 1 teaspoon dried oregano
- 1 teaspoon dried basil
- 1 teaspoon salt
- 1/2 teaspoon black pepper
- 1 cup small mozzarella cheese cubes (about 1/2 inch each)
- 2 cups marinara sauce
- 2 tablespoons olive oil

Instructions:

1. Preheat Oven: Preheat your oven to 400°F (200°C).
2. Prepare Meatball Mixture: In a large mixing bowl, combine ground beef, ground pork, breadcrumbs, grated Parmesan cheese, minced garlic, chopped onion, chopped parsley, egg, dried oregano, dried basil, salt, and black pepper. Mix until all ingredients are well combined.
3. Form Meatballs: Take a small amount of the meat mixture (about 2 tablespoons) and flatten it in your hand. Place a cube of mozzarella cheese in the center and wrap the meat mixture around it, rolling it into a ball. Make sure the cheese is completely covered by the meat to prevent it from oozing out during cooking. Repeat with the remaining meat mixture and cheese cubes.
4. Cook Meatballs: In a large oven-safe skillet, heat olive oil over medium-high heat. Add the meatballs in batches, searing them on all sides until browned. Transfer the seared meatballs to a plate.
5. Bake Meatballs: Once all the meatballs are seared, return them to the skillet. Pour the marinara sauce over the meatballs, ensuring they are evenly coated. Transfer the skillet to the preheated oven and bake for 20-25 minutes, or until the meatballs are cooked through and the cheese inside is melted.
6. Serve: Remove the meatballs from the oven and let them rest for a few minutes. Serve hot, topped with extra marinara sauce and a sprinkle of chopped fresh parsley if desired.

Enjoy your delicious Cheese-Stuffed Meatballs!

Cheese Fondue

Ingredients:

- 1 clove garlic, halved
- 1 cup dry white wine (such as Sauvignon Blanc)
- 1 tablespoon lemon juice
- 2 cups grated Gruyère cheese
- 2 cups grated Emmental cheese
- 1 tablespoon cornstarch
- 1 tablespoon kirsch (cherry brandy, optional)
- Freshly ground black pepper, to taste
- Freshly grated nutmeg, to taste
- Assorted dippers: cubed crusty bread, blanched vegetables (like broccoli, cauliflower, and carrots), apple slices, cooked potatoes, and sausage pieces

Instructions:

1. Prepare Fondue Pot:
    - Rub the inside of a fondue pot or a heavy-bottomed saucepan with the cut sides of the garlic clove to impart flavor. Discard the garlic afterward.
2. Heat Wine and Lemon Juice:
    - Pour the white wine and lemon juice into the pot and heat over medium heat until it is hot but not boiling.
3. Prepare Cheese Mixture:
    - In a medium bowl, toss the grated Gruyère and Emmental cheeses with the cornstarch. This helps to prevent the cheese from clumping together and ensures a smooth fondue.
4. Melt Cheese:
    - Gradually add the cheese mixture to the pot, a handful at a time, stirring constantly in a figure-eight motion. Allow each addition to melt completely before adding the next. Continue this process until all the cheese is melted and the mixture is smooth and creamy.
5. Add Kirsch and Season:
    - Stir in the kirsch, if using, and continue to cook, stirring, until the fondue is smooth and bubbling. Season with freshly ground black pepper and freshly grated nutmeg to taste.
6. Serve:
    - Transfer the pot to a fondue stand or a tabletop burner to keep the fondue warm and melty. Arrange the assorted dippers around the pot and provide fondue forks or skewers for dipping.

Tips:

- Consistency: If the fondue is too thick, add a little more wine. If it's too thin, add a bit more cheese mixed with cornstarch.
- Dippers: Ensure that the dippers are cut into bite-sized pieces for easy dipping.
- Serving: Fondue is best enjoyed immediately, while it is hot and melty.

Enjoy your classic and delicious Cheese Fondue with a variety of tasty dippers!

Cheddar Cheese Soup

Ingredients:

- 4 tablespoons unsalted butter
- 1 medium onion, finely chopped
- 2 cloves garlic, minced
- 2 celery stalks, finely chopped
- 2 medium carrots, finely chopped
- 1/4 cup all-purpose flour
- 3 cups chicken or vegetable broth
- 2 cups whole milk
- 1 cup heavy cream
- 4 cups sharp cheddar cheese, grated
- 1 teaspoon Dijon mustard
- 1/4 teaspoon Worcestershire sauce
- Salt and pepper, to taste
- Fresh chives, chopped (optional, for garnish)
- Croutons or bread for serving

Instructions:

1. Prepare Vegetables:
    - Melt the butter in a large pot over medium heat. Add the finely chopped onion, garlic, celery, and carrots. Cook until the vegetables are softened, about 5-7 minutes.
2. Make Roux:
    - Stir in the flour and cook, stirring constantly, for about 2 minutes until the flour is lightly browned and forms a roux.
3. Add Liquids:
    - Gradually whisk in the chicken or vegetable broth, ensuring there are no lumps. Then add the milk and heavy cream. Bring the mixture to a simmer, stirring occasionally.
4. Cook Soup Base:
    - Reduce the heat to low and let the soup base cook gently for about 10-15 minutes, until it thickens slightly.
5. Add Cheese:
    - Gradually add the grated cheddar cheese to the pot, stirring constantly until the cheese is fully melted and the soup is smooth.
6. Season:
    - Stir in the Dijon mustard and Worcestershire sauce. Season with salt and pepper to taste.
7. Serve:

- Ladle the soup into bowls and garnish with chopped fresh chives if desired. Serve with croutons or bread on the side.

Tips:

- **Consistency:** If the soup is too thick, you can add more broth or milk until it reaches your desired consistency.
- **Cheese:** Use high-quality sharp cheddar cheese for the best flavor.
- **Blending:** For a smoother soup, you can blend the soup base with an immersion blender before adding the cheese.

Enjoy your rich and creamy Cheddar Cheese Soup!

Cheese-Stuffed Pretzels

Ingredients:

Pretzel Dough:

- 1 1/2 cups warm water (110°F or 45°C)
- 2 1/4 teaspoons active dry yeast
- 1 tablespoon granulated sugar
- 4 cups all-purpose flour
- 2 teaspoons salt
- 1/4 cup unsalted butter, melted

Cheese Filling:

- 1 1/2 cups shredded cheddar cheese (or your preferred cheese)

Baking Soda Bath:

- 10 cups water
- 2/3 cup baking soda

Topping:

- 1 egg yolk beaten with 1 tablespoon water (egg wash)
- Coarse sea salt

Instructions:

1. Prepare the Dough:
   - In a large mixing bowl, combine the warm water, yeast, and sugar. Let it sit for about 5 minutes, until the mixture becomes frothy.
   - Add the flour, salt, and melted butter to the yeast mixture. Mix until a dough forms.
   - Knead the dough on a floured surface for about 5-7 minutes, until it is smooth and elastic.
   - Place the dough in a lightly oiled bowl, cover with plastic wrap, and let it rise in a warm place for about 1 hour, or until it has doubled in size.
2. Prepare the Baking Soda Bath:
   - In a large pot, bring 10 cups of water and the baking soda to a boil. Reduce the heat to a simmer while you shape the pretzels.
3. Shape the Pretzels:
   - Preheat your oven to 450°F (230°C). Line a baking sheet with parchment paper.
   - Punch down the risen dough and divide it into 8 equal pieces.
   - Roll each piece into a long rope, about 20 inches in length.

- Flatten each rope and place a line of shredded cheese down the center. Fold the dough over the cheese and pinch the edges tightly to seal, forming a cheese-filled rope.
- Shape each rope into a pretzel by forming a U-shape, crossing the ends over each other, and pressing the ends onto the bottom of the U.
4. Boil the Pretzels:
    - Carefully place each pretzel into the simmering baking soda bath for 30 seconds. Remove with a slotted spoon and place them on the prepared baking sheet.
5. Bake the Pretzels:
    - Brush each pretzel with the egg wash and sprinkle with coarse sea salt.
    - Bake in the preheated oven for 12-15 minutes, or until the pretzels are golden brown.
6. Serve:
    - Let the pretzels cool slightly before serving. Enjoy them warm, with the melted cheese filling inside!

These Cheese-Stuffed Pretzels are perfect for a snack, appetizer, or even a fun party treat. Enjoy!

Grilled Cheese Sandwich

Ingredients:

- 4 slices of bread (sourdough, white, or whole wheat)
- 4 tablespoons unsalted butter, softened
- 2 cups shredded cheese (cheddar, mozzarella, or a blend)
- Optional: 2 slices of cooked bacon, tomato slices, caramelized onions

Instructions:

1. Prepare Bread:
    - Spread a thin layer of softened butter on one side of each slice of bread.
2. Assemble Sandwich:
    - Place one slice of bread, buttered side down, on a cutting board or plate.
    - Evenly sprinkle 1 cup of shredded cheese on the bread.
    - Add any optional ingredients like cooked bacon, tomato slices, or caramelized onions on top of the cheese.
    - Top with another slice of bread, buttered side up.
3. Heat Pan:
    - Heat a skillet or griddle over medium heat until it's hot.
4. Grill Sandwich:
    - Place the assembled sandwich in the hot skillet.
    - Cook for about 3-4 minutes on each side, pressing down gently with a spatula, until the bread is golden brown and crispy and the cheese is melted.
5. Serve:
    - Remove the sandwich from the skillet and let it cool for a minute.
    - Cut the sandwich in half and serve immediately.

Tips:

- Cheese Choice: For a classic taste, use sharp cheddar cheese. For a more gooey texture, try a mix of mozzarella and cheddar.
- Bread Choice: Sourdough or artisan bread can add more flavor and texture.
- Even Melting: If the bread is browning too quickly before the cheese melts, lower the heat and cover the skillet to help the cheese melt.

Enjoy your perfect, melty, and crispy Grilled Cheese Sandwich!

Caprese Salad with Fresh Mozzarella

Ingredients:

- 2 large ripe tomatoes, sliced
- 8 oz (about 225g) fresh mozzarella cheese, sliced
- Fresh basil leaves
- Extra virgin olive oil
- Balsamic glaze (optional)
- Salt and freshly ground black pepper, to taste

Instructions:

1. Prepare Ingredients:
    - Wash and slice the tomatoes into rounds, about 1/4 inch thick.
    - Slice the fresh mozzarella cheese into similar-sized rounds.
2. Assemble Salad:
    - On a serving platter or individual plates, alternate slices of tomato and mozzarella cheese.
    - Tuck fresh basil leaves in between the tomato and cheese slices.
3. Season:
    - Drizzle extra virgin olive oil over the tomato and mozzarella slices.
    - Season with salt and freshly ground black pepper to taste.
4. Optional:
    - If desired, drizzle balsamic glaze over the salad for extra flavor and decoration.
5. Serve:
    - Serve the Caprese Salad immediately as a refreshing appetizer or side dish.

Tips:

- Tomatoes: Choose ripe and juicy tomatoes for the best flavor.
- Mozzarella: Use fresh mozzarella, which is softer and creamier than regular mozzarella.
- Basil: Fresh basil adds a wonderful aromatic flavor to the salad.
- Presentation: Arrange the salad neatly on the plate for an elegant presentation.

Caprese Salad is perfect for summer gatherings or as a light and healthy starter. Enjoy its simplicity and fresh flavors!

Baked Brie with Honey and Nuts

Ingredients:

- 1 wheel of brie cheese (about 8-10 oz)
- 2-3 tablespoons honey
- 1/4 cup chopped nuts (such as pecans, walnuts, or almonds)
- Fresh rosemary sprigs (optional, for garnish)
- Crackers or sliced baguette, for serving

Instructions:

1. Preheat Oven:
    - Preheat your oven to 350°F (175°C).
2. Prepare Brie:
    - Place the wheel of brie cheese on a baking dish or a small oven-safe skillet.
3. Add Toppings:
    - Drizzle the honey over the top of the brie cheese, spreading it evenly with a spoon.
    - Sprinkle the chopped nuts over the honey.
4. Bake:
    - Bake the brie cheese in the preheated oven for about 10-15 minutes, or until the cheese is softened and gooey, and the nuts are lightly toasted. Keep an eye on it to prevent the cheese from melting too much.
5. Serve:
    - Carefully remove the baked brie from the oven and let it cool for a few minutes.
    - Garnish with fresh rosemary sprigs for added flavor and presentation, if desired.
    - Serve warm with crackers or sliced baguette.

Tips:

- Choosing Brie: Opt for a good quality brie cheese that is ripe but not overly runny.
- Honey: Use your favorite honey variety, such as wildflower honey or clover honey, for different flavor profiles.
- Nuts: Toast the nuts lightly beforehand for enhanced flavor and crunch.
- Presentation: Transfer the baked brie to a serving platter for a beautiful presentation, and encourage guests to scoop out the warm, gooey cheese onto their crackers or bread.

This Baked Brie with Honey and Nuts makes a fantastic appetizer for parties or gatherings, combining savory and sweet flavors in each bite. Enjoy!

Cheese and Bacon Stuffed Mushrooms

Ingredients:

- 20 large white mushrooms
- 6 slices bacon, cooked and crumbled
- 4 oz (about 1 cup) cream cheese, softened
- 1/2 cup shredded mozzarella cheese
- 1/4 cup grated Parmesan cheese
- 2 cloves garlic, minced
- 1 tablespoon chopped fresh parsley
- Salt and pepper, to taste
- Olive oil or cooking spray, for greasing

Instructions:

1. Prepare Mushrooms:
    - Preheat your oven to 375°F (190°C). Grease a baking sheet with olive oil or cooking spray.
    - Clean the mushrooms with a damp paper towel to remove any dirt. Remove the stems from the mushrooms and set aside. Place the mushroom caps on the prepared baking sheet, cavity side up.
2. Prepare Filling:
    - In a mixing bowl, combine the cream cheese, shredded mozzarella cheese, grated Parmesan cheese, minced garlic, chopped parsley, crumbled bacon, salt, and pepper. Mix until well combined.
3. Stuff Mushrooms:
    - Spoon a generous amount of the cheese and bacon mixture into each mushroom cap, filling them evenly.
4. Bake:
    - Bake the stuffed mushrooms in the preheated oven for 18-20 minutes, or until the mushrooms are tender and the filling is golden and bubbly.
5. Serve:
    - Remove from the oven and let the stuffed mushrooms cool slightly before serving.

Tips:

- Bacon: Ensure the bacon is cooked until crispy before crumbling.
- Cheese: Feel free to experiment with different types of cheeses such as cheddar or Gruyère for variations in flavor.
- Make Ahead: You can prepare the stuffed mushrooms ahead of time and refrigerate them until ready to bake.

These Cheese and Bacon Stuffed Mushrooms are sure to be a hit at parties or as a delicious appetizer before dinner. Enjoy the savory combination of cheese, bacon, and mushrooms!

Pimento Cheese Spread

Ingredients:

- 8 oz (about 2 cups) sharp cheddar cheese, grated
- 4 oz (about 1 cup) Monterey Jack cheese, grated
- 1/2 cup mayonnaise
- 1/4 cup cream cheese, softened
- 1/4 cup diced pimentos, drained
- 1 tablespoon grated onion
- 1 teaspoon Worcestershire sauce
- 1/2 teaspoon garlic powder
- 1/4 teaspoon cayenne pepper (optional, for a bit of heat)
- Salt and pepper, to taste

Instructions:

1. Prepare Cheese:
    - In a large mixing bowl, combine the grated sharp cheddar cheese and Monterey Jack cheese.
2. Mix Ingredients:
    - Add mayonnaise, softened cream cheese, diced pimentos, grated onion, Worcestershire sauce, garlic powder, cayenne pepper (if using), salt, and pepper to the bowl with the cheeses.
3. Blend Together:
    - Mix all ingredients together until well combined and creamy. You can use a spoon or spatula for this step, or mix with a hand mixer for a smoother consistency.
4. Chill (Optional):
    - For best flavor, cover the bowl with plastic wrap and refrigerate for at least 1 hour before serving. This allows the flavors to meld together.
5. Serve:
    - Once chilled, transfer the pimento cheese spread to a serving bowl.
    - Serve as a spread on sandwiches, crackers, or as a dip with vegetables.

Tips:

- Cheese: Grate the cheese yourself for the best texture and flavor.
- Consistency: If you prefer a thicker spread, adjust the amount of mayonnaise and cream cheese accordingly.
- Variations: Add diced jalapeños for a spicy kick, or smoked paprika for a smoky flavor.

Enjoy your homemade Pimento Cheese Spread as a versatile and delicious addition to any meal or snack!

Cheese Quesadillas

Ingredients:

- 4 large flour tortillas
- 2 cups shredded cheese (cheddar, Monterey Jack, or a blend)
- Optional additions:
    - Sliced jalapeños
    - Chopped bell peppers
    - Cooked chicken or beef strips
    - Chopped onions
    - Sliced tomatoes
    - Fresh cilantro
- Cooking spray or butter

Instructions:

1. Prepare the Tortillas:
    - Lay out the tortillas on a clean surface.
2. Add Cheese and Fillings:
    - Sprinkle shredded cheese evenly over half of each tortilla.
    - If desired, add any optional fillings such as sliced jalapeños, chopped bell peppers, cooked chicken or beef strips, chopped onions, sliced tomatoes, or fresh cilantro.
3. Fold and Press:
    - Fold the tortillas in half over the cheese and fillings to form a half-moon shape.
4. Cook the Quesadillas:
    - Heat a large skillet or griddle over medium heat. Spray with cooking spray or melt a small amount of butter in the skillet.
    - Carefully place the quesadillas in the skillet and cook for about 2-3 minutes on each side, or until they are golden brown and crispy, and the cheese is melted. You may need to press down lightly with a spatula to help seal and cook evenly.
5. Serve:
    - Remove the quesadillas from the skillet and place them on a cutting board. Allow them to cool for a minute, then slice each quesadilla into 2 or 4 wedges.
    - Serve hot, optionally with salsa, guacamole, sour cream, or your favorite dipping sauce on the side.

Tips:

- Cheese: Use a good melting cheese like cheddar or Monterey Jack, or a blend for added flavor.
- Variations: Experiment with different fillings to suit your taste preferences or use leftover meats and vegetables.

- Cooking: Keep an eye on the quesadillas while cooking to ensure they don't burn. Adjust the heat as needed.

Enjoy your homemade cheese quesadillas as a delicious and satisfying meal or snack!

Blue Cheese and Walnut Salad

Ingredients:

- 6 cups mixed salad greens (such as lettuce, arugula, or spinach)
- 1/2 cup walnuts, toasted and chopped
- 1/2 cup crumbled blue cheese (such as Gorgonzola or Roquefort)
- 1/2 cup cherry tomatoes, halved
- 1/4 cup red onion, thinly sliced
- 1/4 cup dried cranberries or fresh berries (optional)

For the Dressing:

- 1/4 cup extra virgin olive oil
- 2 tablespoons balsamic vinegar
- 1 teaspoon Dijon mustard
- 1 teaspoon honey (optional, for sweetness)
- Salt and pepper, to taste

Instructions:

1. Prepare the Dressing:
    - In a small bowl, whisk together the extra virgin olive oil, balsamic vinegar, Dijon mustard, honey (if using), salt, and pepper until well combined. Set aside.
2. Assemble the Salad:
    - In a large salad bowl, combine the mixed salad greens, toasted walnuts, crumbled blue cheese, cherry tomatoes, red onion, and dried cranberries or fresh berries (if using).
3. Dress the Salad:
    - Drizzle the dressing over the salad ingredients, starting with a small amount and adding more as desired. Toss gently to coat the salad evenly with the dressing.
4. Serve:
    - Divide the salad onto individual plates or bowls and serve immediately as a delicious and nutritious meal or side dish.

Tips:

- Toasting Walnuts: To toast walnuts, spread them in a single layer on a baking sheet and bake in a preheated oven at 350°F (175°C) for 8-10 minutes, or until fragrant and lightly golden. Let them cool before chopping and adding to the salad.
- Customization: Feel free to customize the salad with additional ingredients such as grilled chicken, avocado slices, or cucumber for added texture and flavor.

- Storage: Store any leftover salad and dressing separately in airtight containers in the refrigerator. The dressing can be stored for several days, while the assembled salad is best enjoyed fresh.

This Blue Cheese and Walnut Salad is not only delicious but also provides a wonderful blend of flavors and textures. Enjoy it as a light lunch or as a side dish with your favorite main course!

Cheesy Scalloped Potatoes

Ingredients:

- 2 lbs (about 1 kg) potatoes, peeled and thinly sliced (about 1/8 inch thick)
- 2 cups shredded cheddar cheese (or your favorite cheese blend)
- 1 cup grated Parmesan cheese
- 2 cups heavy cream (or half-and-half for a lighter version)
- 4 tablespoons unsalted butter, cut into small pieces
- 2 cloves garlic, minced
- 1 teaspoon dried thyme (or 1 tablespoon fresh thyme leaves)
- Salt and pepper, to taste
- Fresh parsley, chopped (optional, for garnish)

Instructions:

1. Preheat Oven:
    - Preheat your oven to 375°F (190°C). Butter a 9x13-inch baking dish or a similar-sized casserole dish.
2. Layer Potatoes and Cheese:
    - Arrange half of the sliced potatoes in an even layer in the prepared baking dish. Season with salt, pepper, and half of the minced garlic.
    - Sprinkle half of the shredded cheddar cheese and grated Parmesan cheese over the potatoes.
    - Repeat with the remaining sliced potatoes, minced garlic, and cheeses.
3. Add Cream Mixture:
    - In a saucepan, heat the heavy cream over medium heat until warm. Stir in the dried thyme (or fresh thyme leaves), salt, and pepper to taste.
    - Pour the warm cream mixture evenly over the layered potatoes and cheese in the baking dish. Gently press down on the potatoes to ensure they are submerged in the cream.
4. Bake:
    - Dot the top of the potato mixture with small pieces of butter.
    - Cover the baking dish with foil and bake in the preheated oven for 45 minutes. Then, remove the foil and bake for an additional 30-40 minutes, or until the potatoes are tender and the top is golden brown and bubbly.
5. Serve:
    - Remove from the oven and let the cheesy scalloped potatoes cool for a few minutes before serving.
    - Garnish with chopped fresh parsley, if desired, and serve warm as a side dish or a comforting main course.

Tips:

- Potato Slicing: Use a mandoline slicer for evenly thin potato slices, or carefully slice them by hand.
- Cheese: Experiment with different cheese combinations such as Gruyère, Fontina, or even a bit of cream cheese for added richness.
- Make-Ahead: You can assemble the dish up to a day ahead, cover, and refrigerate. Bake as directed when ready to serve.

These Cheesy Scalloped Potatoes are creamy, flavorful, and perfect for family dinners or holiday gatherings. Enjoy the rich comfort of this classic dish!

Cheese-Stuffed Chicken Breast

Ingredients:

- 4 boneless, skinless chicken breasts
- Salt and pepper, to taste
- 1 cup shredded mozzarella cheese (or your preferred melting cheese)
- 1/4 cup grated Parmesan cheese
- 1/2 teaspoon garlic powder
- 1/2 teaspoon paprika
- 1/2 teaspoon dried oregano
- 1/2 teaspoon dried basil
- 1/4 teaspoon onion powder
- 1 tablespoon olive oil
- Fresh parsley, chopped (optional, for garnish)

Instructions:

1. Preheat Oven:
    - Preheat your oven to 375°F (190°C).
2. Prepare Chicken Breasts:
    - Use a sharp knife to cut a pocket horizontally into the thickest part of each chicken breast, being careful not to cut all the way through. Season both sides of the chicken breasts with salt and pepper.
3. Make Cheese Filling:
    - In a small bowl, combine the shredded mozzarella cheese, grated Parmesan cheese, garlic powder, paprika, dried oregano, dried basil, and onion powder.
4. Stuff Chicken Breasts:
    - Stuff each chicken breast with the cheese mixture, dividing it evenly among them. Press the edges of the chicken together to seal the pockets, or use toothpicks to secure if needed.
5. Cook Chicken:
    - Heat olive oil in a large oven-safe skillet over medium-high heat. Add the stuffed chicken breasts and cook for 3-4 minutes per side, or until they are golden brown.
6. Finish in Oven:
    - Transfer the skillet to the preheated oven and bake for 20-25 minutes, or until the chicken reaches an internal temperature of 165°F (74°C) and the cheese is melted and bubbly.
7. Serve:
    - Remove the cheese-stuffed chicken breasts from the oven and let them rest for a few minutes. Garnish with chopped fresh parsley if desired, then slice and serve.

Tips:

- Variations: Feel free to customize the cheese filling with your favorite herbs and spices, or use different types of cheese such as cheddar, provolone, or goat cheese.
- Side Dishes: Serve the cheese-stuffed chicken breast with a side of roasted vegetables, mashed potatoes, or a fresh salad for a complete meal.
- Precaution: If using toothpicks to secure the chicken, remember to remove them before serving.

This cheese-stuffed chicken breast recipe is perfect for a special dinner at home, offering a delicious combination of flavors and textures. Enjoy!

Spinach and Cheese Stuffed Manicotti

Ingredients:

- 1 box (8 ounces) manicotti pasta shells
- 1 tablespoon olive oil
- 1 small onion, finely chopped
- 2 cloves garlic, minced
- 5 ounces fresh spinach, chopped (about 4 cups packed)
- 15 ounces ricotta cheese
- 1 cup shredded mozzarella cheese, divided
- 1/2 cup grated Parmesan cheese, divided
- 1 egg
- 1/2 teaspoon dried oregano
- 1/2 teaspoon dried basil
- Salt and pepper, to taste
- 2 cups marinara sauce
- Fresh basil leaves, chopped (optional, for garnish)

Instructions:

1. Cook Manicotti:
   - Preheat your oven to 350°F (175°C).
   - Cook the manicotti pasta shells according to the package instructions until al dente. Drain and set aside on a clean kitchen towel to cool slightly.
2. Prepare Filling:
   - In a large skillet, heat olive oil over medium heat. Add the chopped onion and cook until softened, about 5 minutes. Add the minced garlic and cook for another 1-2 minutes until fragrant.
   - Add the chopped spinach to the skillet and cook until wilted, about 2-3 minutes. Remove from heat and let it cool slightly.
3. Make Cheese Mixture:
   - In a large bowl, combine the ricotta cheese, 1/2 cup shredded mozzarella cheese, 1/4 cup grated Parmesan cheese, egg, dried oregano, dried basil, salt, and pepper.
   - Add the cooked spinach mixture to the cheese mixture and stir until well combined.
4. Fill Manicotti:
   - Using a small spoon or piping bag, carefully fill each cooked manicotti shell with the spinach and cheese mixture.
5. Assemble and Bake:
   - Spread 1 cup of marinara sauce evenly on the bottom of a 9x13-inch baking dish.
   - Arrange the filled manicotti shells in a single layer over the marinara sauce.

- Pour the remaining marinara sauce over the filled manicotti shells, covering them evenly.
  - Sprinkle the remaining 1/2 cup shredded mozzarella cheese and 1/4 cup grated Parmesan cheese over the top.
6. Bake:
   - Cover the baking dish with aluminum foil and bake in the preheated oven for 25-30 minutes, or until the cheese is melted and bubbly.
7. Serve:
   - Remove from the oven and let the Spinach and Cheese Stuffed Manicotti cool for a few minutes before serving.
   - Garnish with chopped fresh basil leaves, if desired, and serve warm.

Tips:

- Make-Ahead: You can assemble the stuffed manicotti ahead of time and refrigerate until ready to bake. Just add a few extra minutes to the baking time.
- Variations: Feel free to add cooked ground meat such as sausage or ground beef to the cheese mixture for added protein.
- Side Dish: Serve Spinach and Cheese Stuffed Manicotti with a side salad and garlic bread for a complete meal.

Enjoy this Spinach and Cheese Stuffed Manicotti as a comforting and flavorful dish that will impress your family and guests!

Cheese Soufflé

Ingredients:

- 3 tablespoons unsalted butter, plus extra for greasing the soufflé dish
- 3 tablespoons all-purpose flour
- 1 cup milk (whole milk preferred)
- 1/2 teaspoon salt
- 1/4 teaspoon black pepper
- 1/4 teaspoon cayenne pepper (optional, for a bit of heat)
- 1/4 teaspoon nutmeg
- 1 1/2 cups shredded cheese (such as Gruyère, cheddar, or a combination)
- 4 large eggs, separated
- Pinch of cream of tartar (optional, to stabilize egg whites)
- Grated Parmesan cheese, for dusting the soufflé dish

Instructions:

1. **Preheat Oven:**
    - Preheat your oven to 375°F (190°C). Place a baking sheet on the middle rack to heat up (this helps to evenly cook the soufflé).
2. **Prepare Soufflé Dish:**
    - Butter a 6-cup soufflé dish generously. Coat the buttered dish with grated Parmesan cheese, shaking out any excess. This helps the soufflé to rise evenly.
3. **Make Roux:**
    - In a medium saucepan, melt 3 tablespoons of butter over medium heat. Add the flour and whisk continuously for about 2 minutes to cook the flour, but do not let it brown.
4. **Add Milk and Seasonings:**
    - Gradually add the milk to the roux, whisking constantly to prevent lumps. Cook until the mixture thickens and comes to a boil, about 3-5 minutes.
    - Remove from heat and stir in salt, black pepper, cayenne pepper (if using), and nutmeg. Let the mixture cool slightly.
5. **Add Cheese and Egg Yolks:**
    - Stir in the shredded cheese until melted and smooth. Quickly whisk in the egg yolks, one at a time, until well combined.
6. **Beat Egg Whites:**
    - In a clean mixing bowl, beat the egg whites (and cream of tartar, if using) with a hand mixer or stand mixer until stiff peaks form.
7. **Fold Egg Whites into Cheese Mixture:**
    - Gently fold about one-third of the beaten egg whites into the cheese mixture to lighten it. Then, carefully fold in the remaining egg whites until just combined. Be gentle to maintain the airiness.
8. **Bake Soufflé:**

- Pour the soufflé mixture into the prepared soufflé dish, smoothing the top with a spatula. Place the soufflé dish on the preheated baking sheet in the oven.
- Bake for 25-30 minutes, or until the soufflé is puffed up and golden brown on top. Avoid opening the oven door too often during baking, as drafts can cause the soufflé to collapse.
9. Serve Immediately:
    - Remove from the oven and serve the cheese soufflé immediately while it is puffed and airy. Serve as a main dish or a sophisticated side dish.

Tips:

- Cheese: Use a combination of cheeses for a more complex flavor. Gruyère and cheddar are popular choices, but you can also add Parmesan or Swiss.
- Egg Whites: Ensure that your egg whites are beaten to stiff peaks for the best rise and texture of the soufflé.
- Presentation: Soufflés are best served right out of the oven, as they will start to deflate shortly after baking.

Enjoy the decadence and elegance of this cheese soufflé as a special dish for a dinner party or a cozy evening at home!

Cheeseburger Sliders

Ingredients:

- 1 lb ground beef (preferably 80% lean)
- Salt and pepper, to taste
- 1 tablespoon Worcestershire sauce
- 1/2 teaspoon garlic powder
- 1/2 teaspoon onion powder
- 12 slider buns (or dinner rolls, cut in half)
- 6 slices cheddar cheese, cut into quarters (or your favorite cheese)
- Optional toppings:
    - Sliced tomatoes
    - Lettuce leaves
    - Pickles
    - Ketchup
    - Mustard
    - Mayonnaise

Instructions:

1. Preheat Grill or Skillet:
    - Preheat your grill or a large skillet over medium-high heat.
2. Prepare Beef Patties:
    - In a mixing bowl, combine the ground beef, salt, pepper, Worcestershire sauce, garlic powder, and onion powder. Mix gently with your hands until well combined.
    - Divide the mixture into 12 equal portions and shape them into small patties slightly larger than the slider buns, as they will shrink during cooking.
3. Cook Patties:
    - Grill or cook the patties in the skillet for about 3-4 minutes per side, or until they reach an internal temperature of 160°F (71°C) for medium doneness.
    - During the last minute of cooking, place a quarter slice of cheese on each patty and let it melt.
4. Toast Buns:
    - While the patties are cooking, lightly toast the slider buns on the grill or in a separate skillet until they are golden brown.
5. Assemble Sliders:
    - Place each cooked cheeseburger patty on the bottom half of a slider bun.
    - Add your desired toppings such as sliced tomatoes, lettuce leaves, pickles, ketchup, mustard, and mayonnaise.
6. Serve:
    - Place the top half of the slider bun over the toppings.
    - Secure each slider with a toothpick if needed and serve immediately while warm.

Tips:

- Cheese: Feel free to use your favorite cheese such as American, Swiss, or pepper jack for different flavor profiles.
- Variations: Customize your sliders with bacon slices, caramelized onions, avocado slices, or different sauces for added flavor.
- Make-Ahead: You can prepare the patties ahead of time and refrigerate them until ready to cook. Alternatively, cook them in advance and reheat gently before assembling the sliders.

These cheeseburger sliders are sure to be a hit with family and friends, offering the classic flavors of a cheeseburger in a fun and convenient mini size!

Cheese Pizza

Ingredients:

For the Pizza Dough:

- 1 and 1/2 cups warm water (around 110°F or 45°C)
- 2 and 1/4 teaspoons active dry yeast (1 packet)
- 1 tablespoon sugar
- 3 and 1/2 cups all-purpose flour
- 2 tablespoons olive oil
- 1 teaspoon salt

For the Pizza Sauce:

- 1 can (15 oz) tomato sauce
- 1 teaspoon dried oregano
- 1 teaspoon dried basil
- 1/2 teaspoon garlic powder
- Salt and pepper, to taste

For Topping:

- 2 cups shredded mozzarella cheese
- 1/2 cup grated Parmesan cheese
- Fresh basil leaves, torn (optional, for garnish)

Instructions:

1. Prepare the Pizza Dough:

- In a large bowl, combine warm water, sugar, and yeast. Let it sit for about 5-10 minutes until foamy.
- Add olive oil, salt, and flour to the yeast mixture. Stir until a dough forms.
- Knead the dough on a floured surface for about 5-7 minutes until smooth and elastic.
- Place the dough in a greased bowl, cover with a damp cloth, and let it rise in a warm place for 1-2 hours until doubled in size.

2. Make the Pizza Sauce:

- In a small bowl, mix together tomato sauce, dried oregano, dried basil, garlic powder, salt, and pepper. Adjust seasoning to taste.

3. Preheat the Oven:

- Preheat your oven to 475°F (245°C). If you have a pizza stone, place it in the oven to heat up.

4. Roll out the Dough:

    - Once the dough has risen, punch it down and divide it into two equal portions for two 12-inch pizzas.
    - On a lightly floured surface, roll out each portion of dough into a 12-inch circle (or your desired thickness).

5. Assemble the Pizza:

    - Transfer the rolled-out dough to a pizza peel or a baking sheet lined with parchment paper.
    - Spread half of the pizza sauce evenly over the dough, leaving a small border around the edges.
    - Sprinkle half of the shredded mozzarella cheese and grated Parmesan cheese over the sauce.

6. Bake the Pizza:

    - Carefully slide the pizza (on the parchment paper if using a baking sheet) onto the preheated pizza stone or place the baking sheet directly into the oven.
    - Bake for 10-12 minutes, or until the crust is golden brown and the cheese is melted and bubbly.

7. Serve:

    - Remove the pizza from the oven and let it cool for a few minutes.
    - Garnish with fresh torn basil leaves, if desired.
    - Slice and serve hot!

Tips:

- Variations: Customize your cheese pizza by adding toppings like pepperoni, mushrooms, bell peppers, onions, or olives.
- Pizza Stone: Using a pizza stone helps to create a crispier crust. Preheat it in the oven before sliding the pizza onto it.
- Make-Ahead: You can make the pizza dough ahead of time and refrigerate or freeze it until ready to use. Allow it to come to room temperature before rolling out.

Enjoy making and savoring your homemade cheese pizza, perfect for any occasion!

Ricotta Cheese Pancakes

Ingredients:

- 1 cup ricotta cheese
- 3/4 cup all-purpose flour
- 2 tablespoons granulated sugar
- 1 teaspoon baking powder
- 1/2 teaspoon baking soda
- 1/4 teaspoon salt
- 2 large eggs, separated
- 1/2 cup milk
- 1 teaspoon vanilla extract
- Butter or cooking spray, for cooking
- Optional toppings: fresh berries, maple syrup, honey, powdered sugar

Instructions:

1. Prepare the Batter:
   - In a large mixing bowl, combine the ricotta cheese, egg yolks, milk, and vanilla extract. Mix until well combined.
2. Mix Dry Ingredients:
   - In a separate bowl, whisk together the flour, sugar, baking powder, baking soda, and salt.
3. Combine Wet and Dry Ingredients:
   - Gradually add the dry ingredients to the ricotta mixture, stirring until just combined. Be careful not to overmix; it's okay if the batter is slightly lumpy.
4. Whip Egg Whites:
   - In another clean bowl, using a hand mixer or a stand mixer with the whisk attachment, beat the egg whites until stiff peaks form.
5. Fold in Egg Whites:
   - Gently fold the beaten egg whites into the pancake batter until just incorporated. This will help to lighten the batter and create fluffy pancakes.
6. Cook the Pancakes:
   - Heat a large non-stick skillet or griddle over medium heat. Add a small amount of butter or coat with cooking spray.
   - Pour about 1/4 cup of batter for each pancake onto the skillet. Cook for 2-3 minutes, or until bubbles form on the surface and the edges look set.
7. Flip and Cook:
   - Carefully flip the pancakes with a spatula and cook for another 1-2 minutes, or until golden brown and cooked through.
8. Serve:
   - Transfer the cooked pancakes to a plate and keep warm. Repeat with the remaining batter.

- Serve the ricotta cheese pancakes warm with your favorite toppings such as fresh berries, maple syrup, honey, or powdered sugar.

Tips:

- Ricotta Texture: For a smoother texture, you can blend the ricotta cheese in a food processor before mixing it with other ingredients.
- Cooking: Adjust the heat as needed to prevent pancakes from burning. You may need to lower the heat slightly after the first batch.
- Storage: Leftover pancakes can be stored in an airtight container in the refrigerator for a few days or frozen for longer storage. Reheat in the toaster or microwave before serving.

Enjoy these fluffy and flavorful ricotta cheese pancakes as a delicious breakfast or brunch treat!

Cheese-Stuffed Jalapeños

Ingredients:

- 12 fresh jalapeño peppers
- 8 oz cream cheese, softened
- 1 cup shredded cheddar cheese (or your favorite melting cheese)
- 1/2 teaspoon garlic powder
- 1/2 teaspoon onion powder
- 1/4 teaspoon paprika
- Salt and pepper, to taste
- 6 slices bacon, cut in half crosswise (optional)
- Toothpicks, for securing jalapeños (if using bacon)

Instructions:

1. Prepare Jalapeños:
   - Preheat your oven to 375°F (190°C). Line a baking sheet with parchment paper.
   - Cut each jalapeño in half lengthwise and use a spoon to scoop out the seeds and membranes. Wear gloves or wash hands thoroughly afterward to avoid irritation from the jalapeño oils.
2. Make Cheese Filling:
   - In a mixing bowl, combine the softened cream cheese, shredded cheddar cheese, garlic powder, onion powder, paprika, salt, and pepper. Mix until smooth and well combined.
3. Stuff Jalapeños:
   - Spoon the cheese mixture evenly into each jalapeño half, pressing gently to fill.
4. Wrap with Bacon (Optional):
   - If using bacon, wrap each stuffed jalapeño half with a half slice of bacon. Secure the bacon with toothpicks, if needed.
5. Bake:
   - Arrange the stuffed jalapeños on the prepared baking sheet. Bake in the preheated oven for 20-25 minutes, or until the jalapeños are tender and the cheese is melted and bubbly.
6. Serve:
   - Remove from the oven and let cool slightly before serving. If desired, garnish with chopped fresh cilantro or green onions.

Tips:

- Spice Level: Adjust the heat of the jalapeños by removing more or fewer seeds and membranes. Leaving some seeds will make them spicier.

- Variations: Experiment with different cheeses such as pepper jack, mozzarella, or a cheese blend. You can also add chopped cooked bacon or sausage to the cheese mixture for added flavor.
- Grilling Option: Instead of baking, you can also grill the cheese-stuffed jalapeños on a preheated grill until the jalapeños are tender and the cheese is melted.

These cheese-stuffed jalapeños are perfect for parties, game days, or anytime you crave a flavorful and slightly spicy appetizer. Enjoy them hot and gooey straight from the oven!

Feta and Spinach Stuffed Phyllo Pastries

Ingredients:

- 1 package (16 oz) frozen phyllo dough, thawed
- 1/2 cup (1 stick) unsalted butter, melted
- 1 lb fresh spinach, washed and chopped
- 1 cup crumbled feta cheese
- 1/2 cup ricotta cheese
- 1/4 cup grated Parmesan cheese
- 1 small onion, finely chopped
- 2 cloves garlic, minced
- 2 tablespoons olive oil
- 1/2 teaspoon dried dill (or 1 tablespoon fresh dill, chopped)
- Salt and pepper, to taste
- 1 egg, beaten (for brushing)

Instructions:

1. Prepare the Spinach Filling:
    - In a large skillet, heat olive oil over medium heat. Add chopped onion and cook until softened, about 5 minutes.
    - Add minced garlic and cook for another 1-2 minutes until fragrant.
    - Add chopped spinach to the skillet in batches, stirring until wilted. Cook for about 5-7 minutes until most of the liquid from the spinach has evaporated.
    - Remove from heat and let the spinach mixture cool slightly.
2. Make the Cheese Filling:
    - In a mixing bowl, combine crumbled feta cheese, ricotta cheese, grated Parmesan cheese, dried dill, salt, and pepper.
    - Add the cooked spinach mixture to the cheese mixture and stir until well combined. Taste and adjust seasoning if needed.
3. Prepare the Phyllo Dough:
    - Preheat your oven to 375°F (190°C). Line a baking sheet with parchment paper.
    - Carefully unroll the thawed phyllo dough sheets. Cover them with a damp towel to prevent drying out while assembling the pastries.
4. Assemble the Pastries:
    - Place one sheet of phyllo dough on a clean, flat surface and brush it lightly with melted butter. Layer another sheet of phyllo dough on top and brush with butter again.
    - Cut the layered phyllo dough into strips about 3 inches wide and 12 inches long.
    - Place a spoonful of the spinach and cheese filling at the end of each strip of phyllo dough.

- Fold one corner of the phyllo dough over the filling to form a triangle, continuing to fold the strip in a triangle shape until you reach the end. Press the edges to seal the pastry.
      - Repeat with the remaining phyllo dough and filling.
   5. Bake the Pastries:
      - Place the stuffed phyllo pastries on the prepared baking sheet. Brush the tops with beaten egg to give them a golden color when baked.
      - Bake in the preheated oven for 20-25 minutes, or until the pastries are golden brown and crisp.
   6. Serve:
      - Remove from the oven and let the pastries cool slightly before serving.
      - Serve warm as an appetizer or snack, garnished with fresh dill or parsley if desired.

Tips:

- Phyllo Handling: Work quickly with phyllo dough and keep it covered with a damp towel to prevent drying out.
- Make-Ahead: You can assemble the stuffed pastries ahead of time and refrigerate them until ready to bake. Brush with melted butter and egg just before baking.
- Variations: Add chopped fresh herbs like parsley or mint to the filling for extra flavor. You can also incorporate pine nuts or diced sun-dried tomatoes for a twist.

These feta and spinach stuffed phyllo pastries are crispy on the outside and bursting with savory goodness inside, making them a perfect appetizer for any occasion. Enjoy the flavors of Greece with every bite!

Cheese and Broccoli Casserole

Ingredients:

- 4 cups fresh broccoli florets (about 1 lb)
- 2 tablespoons unsalted butter
- 2 tablespoons all-purpose flour
- 1 cup milk
- 1 cup shredded cheddar cheese
- 1/2 cup shredded mozzarella cheese
- Salt and pepper, to taste
- 1/4 teaspoon garlic powder
- 1/4 teaspoon onion powder
- 1/4 teaspoon paprika
- 1/2 cup breadcrumbs
- 2 tablespoons grated Parmesan cheese
- 2 tablespoons melted butter

Instructions:

1. Preheat Oven:
    - Preheat your oven to 350°F (175°C). Lightly grease a 2-quart baking dish with butter or cooking spray.
2. Cook Broccoli:
    - Bring a large pot of salted water to a boil. Add the broccoli florets and blanch for 2-3 minutes until bright green and slightly tender. Drain well and set aside.
3. Make Cheese Sauce:
    - In a medium saucepan, melt 2 tablespoons of butter over medium heat. Stir in the flour and cook for 1-2 minutes until bubbly and golden.
    - Gradually whisk in the milk, stirring constantly until smooth and thickened.
    - Reduce heat to low and add the shredded cheddar cheese and mozzarella cheese, stirring until melted and smooth. Season with salt, pepper, garlic powder, onion powder, and paprika.
4. Assemble Casserole:
    - Place the blanched broccoli florets in the prepared baking dish. Pour the cheese sauce evenly over the broccoli, coating all pieces.
5. Prepare Topping:
    - In a small bowl, combine the breadcrumbs, grated Parmesan cheese, and melted butter. Mix until well combined.
6. Bake:
    - Sprinkle the breadcrumb topping evenly over the cheese and broccoli mixture in the baking dish.
    - Bake in the preheated oven for 25-30 minutes, or until the casserole is bubbly and the top is golden brown.

7. Serve:
    - Remove from the oven and let the casserole cool for a few minutes before serving.
    - Serve warm as a side dish or a main course, garnished with additional Parmesan cheese if desired.

Tips:

- Variations: Add cooked diced chicken, ham, or bacon to the casserole for a heartier dish.
- Vegetarian Option: Substitute vegetable broth for chicken broth to keep it vegetarian.
- Make-Ahead: You can assemble the casserole ahead of time and refrigerate it, covered, until ready to bake. Add the breadcrumb topping just before baking.

This cheese and broccoli casserole is a perfect comfort food dish that combines creamy cheese sauce with nutritious broccoli, making it a favorite for family dinners or potlucks. Enjoy the rich flavors and satisfying textures in every bite!

Cheese and Herb Focaccia

Ingredients:

For the Dough:

- 3 cups all-purpose flour
- 1 teaspoon salt
- 1 tablespoon granulated sugar
- 1 tablespoon active dry yeast
- 1 cup warm water (about 110°F or 45°C)
- 3 tablespoons olive oil, divided
- 1/2 cup shredded mozzarella cheese (or your favorite cheese)
- 1/4 cup grated Parmesan cheese

For the Topping:

- 2 tablespoons olive oil
- 2-3 cloves garlic, minced
- 1 tablespoon fresh rosemary, chopped (or 1 teaspoon dried rosemary)
- 1 tablespoon fresh thyme leaves (or 1 teaspoon dried thyme)
- 1/2 cup shredded mozzarella cheese
- 1/4 cup grated Parmesan cheese
- Coarse sea salt, for sprinkling

Instructions:

1. Prepare the Dough:
    - In a large mixing bowl, combine the flour, salt, and sugar. Make a well in the center.
    - In a small bowl, dissolve the yeast in warm water and let it sit for 5-10 minutes until foamy.
    - Pour the yeast mixture and 2 tablespoons of olive oil into the well of the flour mixture. Stir until a dough forms.
    - Turn the dough out onto a lightly floured surface and knead for about 5-7 minutes until smooth and elastic.
    - Place the dough in a greased bowl, cover with a damp towel, and let it rise in a warm place for about 1 hour or until doubled in size.
2. Prepare the Focaccia:
    - Preheat your oven to 425°F (220°C). Line a baking sheet with parchment paper.
    - Punch down the risen dough and transfer it to the prepared baking sheet. Gently stretch or roll the dough to fit the size of the baking sheet, about 1/2 inch thick.
3. Add Toppings:
    - Using your fingertips, make indentations all over the surface of the dough.

- In a small bowl, combine 2 tablespoons of olive oil with minced garlic, chopped rosemary, and thyme leaves. Brush this mixture evenly over the surface of the dough.
        - Sprinkle shredded mozzarella cheese and grated Parmesan cheese evenly over the top of the dough. Press them lightly into the indentations.
        - Sprinkle with coarse sea salt for added flavor.
    4. Bake the Focaccia:
        - Bake in the preheated oven for 15-20 minutes, or until the focaccia is golden brown and cooked through.
    5. Serve:
        - Remove from the oven and let the focaccia cool slightly on a wire rack.
        - Cut into squares or wedges and serve warm. Enjoy the cheesy, herb-infused goodness!

Tips:

- Cheese Variations: Feel free to experiment with different cheeses such as cheddar, Gruyère, or a blend of cheeses for different flavor profiles.
- Herb Substitutions: If you prefer other herbs, you can use fresh basil, parsley, or oregano instead of rosemary and thyme.
- Storage: Store leftover focaccia in an airtight container at room temperature for up to 2 days. Reheat in the oven or toaster oven before serving.

This cheese and herb focaccia is perfect as an appetizer, side dish, or even as a light meal with a salad. The combination of savory cheese and fragrant herbs makes it a crowd-pleaser for any occasion!

Cheese Enchiladas

Ingredients:

For the Enchilada Sauce:

- 2 tablespoons vegetable oil
- 2 tablespoons all-purpose flour
- 4 tablespoons chili powder
- 1/2 teaspoon cayenne pepper (optional, for extra heat)
- 1/2 teaspoon ground cumin
- 1/2 teaspoon garlic powder
- 1/4 teaspoon onion powder
- 1/4 teaspoon dried oregano
- 2 cups chicken or vegetable broth
- 1 can (8 oz) tomato sauce
- Salt and pepper, to taste

For the Cheese Enchiladas:

- 2 cups shredded cheese (cheddar, Monterey Jack, or a blend)
- 12 corn tortillas (or flour tortillas)
- 1/4 cup chopped fresh cilantro (optional, for garnish)
- Sour cream, sliced jalapeños, diced onions (optional, for serving)

Instructions:

1. Prepare the Enchilada Sauce:
    - Heat vegetable oil in a saucepan over medium heat. Stir in flour and cook for 1 minute to make a roux.
    - Add chili powder, cayenne pepper (if using), cumin, garlic powder, onion powder, and dried oregano. Cook for another minute to toast the spices.
    - Gradually whisk in chicken or vegetable broth and tomato sauce until smooth.
    - Bring to a simmer and cook for 10-15 minutes, stirring occasionally, until the sauce thickens. Season with salt and pepper to taste. Remove from heat and set aside.
2. Prepare the Cheese Enchiladas:
    - Preheat your oven to 350°F (175°C). Lightly grease a 9x13-inch baking dish.
    - In a mixing bowl, combine shredded cheese and 1/2 cup of the enchilada sauce. This will be the filling for the enchiladas.
    - Warm the tortillas slightly in the microwave or on a skillet until they are pliable.
3. Assemble and Roll the Enchiladas:
    - Spoon a small amount of the enchilada sauce onto each tortilla and spread it evenly.

- Place a generous amount of the cheese filling (about 2-3 tablespoons) in the center of each tortilla.
    - Roll up the tortilla tightly and place seam-side down in the prepared baking dish. Repeat with the remaining tortillas and filling.
4. Top with Enchilada Sauce:
    - Pour the remaining enchilada sauce over the rolled tortillas, spreading it evenly to cover them.
    - Sprinkle any remaining cheese on top of the enchiladas.
5. Bake the Enchiladas:
    - Cover the baking dish with aluminum foil and bake in the preheated oven for 20-25 minutes, or until the enchiladas are heated through and the cheese is melted.
6. Serve:
    - Remove from the oven and let the enchiladas cool for a few minutes before serving.
    - Garnish with chopped fresh cilantro, if desired.
    - Serve warm with sour cream, sliced jalapeños, diced onions, or your favorite toppings.

Tips:

- **Variations:** You can add cooked chicken, beef, or beans to the cheese filling for added protein and flavor.
- **Make-Ahead:** Assemble the enchiladas ahead of time and refrigerate them, covered, until ready to bake. Add extra baking time if baking from cold.
- **Corn vs. Flour Tortillas:** Corn tortillas are traditional for enchiladas and provide a more authentic flavor, but you can use flour tortillas if preferred.

These cheese enchiladas are flavorful, cheesy, and perfect for a satisfying meal. They are great for family dinners or gatherings, and you can customize them with your favorite toppings for a personal touch!

Gouda and Apple Grilled Cheese

Ingredients:

- 4 slices of bread (choose your favorite type, such as sourdough or whole wheat)
- 4 oz Gouda cheese, sliced or grated
- 1 apple (such as Granny Smith or Honeycrisp), thinly sliced
- Butter, softened (for spreading)
- Honey (optional, for drizzling)

Instructions:

1. Prepare the Sandwich:
    - Heat a non-stick skillet or griddle over medium heat.
    - Butter one side of each slice of bread.
2. Assemble the Sandwich:
    - Place two slices of bread, buttered side down, on a clean surface.
    - Layer the Gouda cheese slices evenly on top of the bread slices.
    - Arrange the apple slices over the cheese.
3. Grill the Sandwich:
    - Top each sandwich with the remaining slices of bread, buttered side facing up.
    - Carefully transfer the sandwiches to the preheated skillet or griddle.
    - Grill for 3-4 minutes on each side, or until the bread is golden brown and the cheese is melted.
    - If desired, press down gently on the sandwiches with a spatula to ensure even cooking and melting.
4. Serve:
    - Remove the grilled cheese sandwiches from the skillet or griddle.
    - Optionally, drizzle a little honey over the apple slices before serving for added sweetness.
    - Cut the sandwiches in half diagonally and serve hot.

Tips:

- Variations: You can add a thin layer of Dijon mustard or mayonnaise to the inside of the bread slices for extra flavor. Additionally, adding a few slices of cooked bacon or prosciutto can complement the flavors well.
- Apples: Experiment with different types of apples to find your favorite combination of sweetness and tartness.
- Cheese: If Gouda is not available, you can substitute it with another melting cheese like Swiss or Havarti.

This Gouda and apple grilled cheese sandwich is a delicious twist on a classic comfort food, perfect for a quick lunch or a cozy dinner. Enjoy the gooey cheese and crisp apple slices melded together between perfectly toasted bread!

Cheese-Stuffed Burger

Ingredients:

- 1 lb ground beef (preferably 80% lean)
- Salt and pepper, to taste
- 4 slices of cheese (cheddar, American, Swiss, or your favorite melting cheese)
- Burger buns
- Optional toppings (lettuce, tomato, onion, pickles, etc.)
- Condiments (ketchup, mustard, mayonnaise, etc.)

Instructions:

1. Prepare the Patties:
   - Divide the ground beef into 8 equal portions (about 2 oz each).
   - Flatten each portion into a thin patty, making sure they are slightly larger than the size of your cheese slices.
   - Season both sides of the patties with salt and pepper.
2. Assemble the Cheese-Stuffed Burgers:
   - Place a slice of cheese in the center of 4 of the patties.
   - Top each cheese-topped patty with another patty.
   - Press the edges together firmly to seal, ensuring no cheese is exposed.
3. Cook the Burgers:
   - Heat a grill, grill pan, or skillet over medium-high heat.
   - Cook the burgers for about 4-5 minutes per side, or until they reach your desired level of doneness (internal temperature of 160°F for medium).
   - If using a grill, you can close the lid to help melt the cheese faster.
4. Toast the Buns:
   - While the burgers are cooking, lightly toast the burger buns on the grill or in a toaster.
5. Assemble the Burgers:
   - Place each cooked burger on a toasted bun.
   - Add your favorite toppings and condiments.
6. Serve:
   - Serve the cheese-stuffed burgers immediately while hot and enjoy the melted cheese center with every bite!

Tips:

- Cheese Variations: Experiment with different types of cheese for the stuffing, such as pepper jack, blue cheese, or mozzarella, depending on your preference for flavor and meltability.
- Handling Patties: Be gentle when forming the patties around the cheese to prevent the cheese from leaking out during cooking.

- Cooking Options: Burgers can also be cooked indoors on a grill pan or skillet if an outdoor grill is not available.

This cheese-stuffed burger recipe will surely satisfy your burger cravings with its juicy meat and gooey cheese center. Customize it with your favorite toppings and enjoy a delicious homemade burger experience!

Cheese and Tomato Tart

Ingredients:

For the Tart Crust:

- 1 sheet of puff pastry, thawed (about 9-10 inches square)
- Flour, for dusting

For the Filling:

- 1 cup shredded cheese (such as Gruyère, cheddar, or mozzarella)
- 2-3 medium tomatoes, thinly sliced
- 1/4 cup grated Parmesan cheese
- 1/4 cup chopped fresh basil leaves
- Salt and pepper, to taste
- Olive oil, for drizzling

Instructions:

1. Preheat Oven:
    - Preheat your oven to 400°F (200°C). Line a baking sheet with parchment paper.
2. Prepare the Tart Crust:
    - Lightly flour a clean surface and roll out the puff pastry sheet into a rectangle, about 12x8 inches or to fit your baking sheet.
    - Transfer the rolled-out pastry sheet onto the prepared baking sheet.
3. Assemble the Tart:
    - Sprinkle the shredded cheese evenly over the puff pastry, leaving about a 1-inch border around the edges.
    - Arrange the thinly sliced tomatoes on top of the cheese, overlapping slightly.
    - Season the tomatoes with salt and pepper to taste.
    - Sprinkle grated Parmesan cheese over the tomatoes.
    - Fold the edges of the puff pastry over the tomatoes, creating a rustic border.
4. Bake the Tart:
    - Drizzle olive oil lightly over the tomatoes and pastry crust.
    - Bake in the preheated oven for 20-25 minutes, or until the pastry is golden brown and crispy, and the tomatoes are tender.
5. Finish and Serve:
    - Remove the tart from the oven and let it cool slightly on a wire rack.
    - Sprinkle chopped fresh basil leaves over the tart before serving.
6. Serve:
    - Slice the cheese and tomato tart into squares or rectangles.
    - Serve warm or at room temperature as an appetizer, side dish, or light meal.

Tips:

- Tomato Selection: Use ripe tomatoes for the best flavor and texture. Roma tomatoes or heirloom varieties work well.
- Cheese Options: Feel free to experiment with different cheeses. In addition to the shredded cheese, you can crumble some goat cheese or feta on top for added tanginess.
- Variations: Add thinly sliced onions, garlic, or fresh herbs like thyme or rosemary to enhance the flavors of the tart.

This cheese and tomato tart is simple to make yet impressively flavorful. It's perfect for showcasing the delicious combination of tomatoes and cheese in a flaky puff pastry crust. Enjoy it as a versatile dish for any occasion!

Parmesan-Crusted Chicken

Ingredients:

- 4 boneless, skinless chicken breasts
- Salt and pepper, to taste
- 1 cup grated Parmesan cheese
- 1 cup breadcrumbs (panko breadcrumbs work well for extra crunch)
- 1 teaspoon garlic powder
- 1 teaspoon dried oregano
- 1/2 teaspoon paprika
- 2 eggs, beaten
- Cooking spray or olive oil

Instructions:

1. Preheat Oven:
   - Preheat your oven to 400°F (200°C). Line a baking sheet with parchment paper or foil and lightly grease with cooking spray or olive oil.
2. Prepare the Chicken:
   - Season both sides of the chicken breasts with salt and pepper.
3. Coat the Chicken:
   - In a shallow bowl or dish, combine grated Parmesan cheese, breadcrumbs, garlic powder, dried oregano, and paprika. Mix well.
   - Dip each chicken breast into the beaten eggs, allowing excess egg to drip off.
   - Press each chicken breast into the Parmesan breadcrumb mixture, coating both sides evenly and pressing gently to adhere.
4. Bake the Chicken:
   - Place the coated chicken breasts on the prepared baking sheet.
   - Lightly spray the tops of the chicken breasts with cooking spray or drizzle with olive oil to help them brown.
   - Bake in the preheated oven for 20-25 minutes, or until the chicken is cooked through (internal temperature should reach 165°F or 75°C) and the coating is golden and crispy.
5. Serve:
   - Remove from the oven and let the Parmesan-crusted chicken rest for a few minutes.
   - Serve hot, garnished with fresh herbs like parsley if desired.

Tips:

- Chicken Thickness: If your chicken breasts are very thick, you can pound them to an even thickness (about 1/2 to 3/4 inch) before coating and baking to ensure even cooking.

- Variations: You can add additional seasonings to the breadcrumb mixture such as Italian seasoning, thyme, or rosemary for extra flavor.
- Side Dish Ideas: Serve Parmesan-crusted chicken with a side of vegetables, pasta, or a fresh salad for a complete meal.

This Parmesan-crusted chicken recipe is sure to become a favorite for its crispy exterior and juicy interior. It's perfect for a family dinner or when you want to impress with a simple yet flavorful dish!

Cheese-Stuffed Peppers

Ingredients:

- 4 large bell peppers (any color)
- 1 cup cooked rice (white or brown)
- 1 cup shredded cheese (such as cheddar, mozzarella, or a blend)
- 1/2 cup diced tomatoes
- 1/4 cup chopped fresh parsley (or cilantro)
- 1/4 cup diced onion
- 2 cloves garlic, minced
- 1 tablespoon olive oil
- 1 teaspoon dried oregano
- 1/2 teaspoon paprika
- Salt and pepper, to taste
- Optional: 1/4 cup breadcrumbs for topping

Instructions:

1. Preheat Oven:Three-Cheese Omelet
   - Preheat your oven to 375°F (190°C). Lightly grease a baking dish large enough to hold the peppers.
2. Prepare the Peppers:
   - Cut the tops off the bell peppers and remove the seeds and membranes from inside. Rinse them under cold water and pat dry with paper towels.
   - If necessary, trim the bottoms of the peppers slightly so that they stand upright in the baking dish without tipping over.
3. Prepare the Filling:
   - In a skillet, heat olive oil over medium heat. Add diced onion and minced garlic, cooking until softened and fragrant, about 3-4 minutes.
   - Add diced tomatoes, cooked rice, dried oregano, paprika, salt, and pepper. Stir and cook for another 2-3 minutes until heated through.
   - Remove from heat and let cool slightly.
4. Stuff the Peppers:
   - In a mixing bowl, combine the cooked rice mixture with shredded cheese and chopped parsley (or cilantro). Mix well.
   - Spoon the filling evenly into each bell pepper, pressing gently to pack it in. Fill the peppers to the top.
5. Bake the Stuffed Peppers:
   - Place the stuffed peppers upright in the prepared baking dish.
   - If desired, sprinkle breadcrumbs over the tops of the stuffed peppers for a crunchy topping.
   - Cover the baking dish with foil and bake in the preheated oven for 30-35 minutes.

- Remove the foil and bake for an additional 10-15 minutes, or until the peppers are tender and the filling is heated through and lightly browned on top.
6. Serve:
    - Remove from the oven and let the stuffed peppers cool slightly before serving.
    - Garnish with additional chopped parsley or cilantro if desired.
    - Serve hot as a delicious appetizer, side dish, or main course.

Tips:

- Cheese Variations: Feel free to experiment with different cheeses such as feta, goat cheese, or pepper jack for different flavors.
- Vegetarian Option: You can omit the rice and add more vegetables like mushrooms, zucchini, or corn to the filling for a vegetarian version.
- Make-Ahead: You can assemble the stuffed peppers ahead of time and refrigerate them, covered, until ready to bake. Add extra baking time if baking from cold.

These cheese-stuffed peppers are hearty, flavorful, and satisfying. They make a great addition to any meal and are sure to be enjoyed by everyone at the table!

Three-Cheese Omelet

Ingredients:

- 3 large eggs
- 1/4 cup shredded cheddar cheese
- 1/4 cup shredded mozzarella cheese
- 1/4 cup crumbled feta cheese
- Salt and pepper, to taste
- 1 tablespoon butter or cooking oil
- Optional fillings: diced ham, cooked bacon, sautéed vegetables (such as spinach, mushrooms, bell peppers), chopped herbs (like parsley or chives)

Instructions:

1. Prepare the Eggs:
   - Crack the eggs into a bowl and whisk them together until well combined. Season with salt and pepper to taste.
2. Heat the Pan:
   - Heat a non-stick skillet over medium heat. Add butter or cooking oil and swirl to coat the pan evenly.
3. Cook the Omelet:
   - Pour the whisked eggs into the heated skillet. Allow the eggs to cook undisturbed for about 1-2 minutes until the edges begin to set.
4. Add Cheese and Fillings:
   - Sprinkle the shredded cheddar, mozzarella, and crumbled feta cheeses evenly over one half of the omelet.
   - If using any optional fillings (like diced ham or sautéed vegetables), add them on top of the cheeses.
5. Fold the Omelet:
   - Using a spatula, gently lift the unfilled side of the omelet and fold it over the side with the cheese and fillings. Press gently with the spatula to seal.
6. Finish Cooking:
   - Cook the omelet for another 1-2 minutes, or until the cheese is melted and the omelet is cooked through to your desired doneness.
7. Serve:
   - Slide the omelet onto a plate. Optionally, garnish with chopped herbs such as parsley or chives.
   - Serve hot, either folded or rolled, with toast, fresh fruit, or a side salad.

Tips:

- Cheese Variations: Feel free to use your favorite cheeses or a different combination such as Swiss, Gruyère, or goat cheese.

- Customization: Add or substitute fillings according to your preference. Ensure that any fillings are cooked or pre-cooked before adding to the omelet.
- Technique: For a fluffy omelet, avoid stirring the eggs too much once they're in the pan. Let them set and cook gently.

This three-cheese omelet is a delicious and satisfying breakfast option that can be easily customized with your favorite ingredients. Enjoy the creamy, cheesy goodness in every bite!

Cheesy Garlic Bread

Ingredients:

- 1 loaf of French bread or Italian bread
- 1/2 cup unsalted butter, softened
- 4 cloves garlic, minced (adjust to taste)
- 1/4 cup grated Parmesan cheese
- 1 cup shredded mozzarella cheese (or your favorite melting cheese)
- 1 tablespoon chopped fresh parsley (optional)
- Salt and pepper, to taste

Instructions:

1. Preheat Oven:
    - Preheat your oven to 375°F (190°C). Line a baking sheet with parchment paper or aluminum foil.
2. Prepare the Garlic Butter:
    - In a small bowl, mix together the softened butter and minced garlic until well combined. Add salt and pepper to taste.
3. Prepare the Bread:
    - Slice the loaf of bread in half lengthwise to create two long halves.
    - Place the bread halves cut-side up on the prepared baking sheet.
4. Spread the Garlic Butter:
    - Spread the garlic butter evenly over the cut sides of the bread halves. Use all of the garlic butter mixture.
5. Add Cheese:
    - Sprinkle grated Parmesan cheese evenly over the garlic buttered bread.
    - Spread shredded mozzarella cheese (or your choice of melting cheese) evenly over the top.
6. Bake the Garlic Bread:
    - Place the baking sheet in the preheated oven and bake for 12-15 minutes, or until the cheese is melted and bubbly, and the edges of the bread are crispy and golden brown.
7. Garnish and Serve:
    - Remove the cheesy garlic bread from the oven.
    - Optional: Garnish with chopped fresh parsley for added freshness and color.
8. Slice and Enjoy:
    - Slice the cheesy garlic bread into pieces and serve hot.
    - Serve as a side dish with pasta, soup, or as an appetizer for parties and gatherings.

Tips:

- Variations: Add a sprinkle of Italian seasoning or red pepper flakes for extra flavor. You can also experiment with different cheeses like cheddar, provolone, or a blend of cheeses.
- Customization: For a twist, you can add toppings like sliced tomatoes, cooked bacon bits, or chopped herbs before adding the cheese.
- Storage: Store any leftover cheesy garlic bread in an airtight container in the refrigerator. Reheat in the oven to maintain its crispiness.

This cheesy garlic bread recipe is sure to be a hit with its gooey cheese, savory garlic butter, and crispy bread. It's perfect for any occasion and is guaranteed to disappear quickly!

Cheese and Herb Scones

Ingredients:

- 2 cups all-purpose flour
- 2 teaspoons baking powder
- 1/2 teaspoon baking soda
- 1/2 teaspoon salt
- 1/2 cup cold unsalted butter, cut into small cubes
- 1 cup grated cheddar cheese (sharp or mild)
- 2 tablespoons chopped fresh herbs (such as parsley, chives, or thyme)
- 1/2 cup plain Greek yogurt (or sour cream)
- 1/2 cup milk
- 1 egg, beaten (for egg wash)
- Additional grated cheese and herbs for topping (optional)

Instructions:

1. Preheat Oven:
    - Preheat your oven to 400°F (200°C). Line a baking sheet with parchment paper or lightly grease it.
2. Prepare the Dough:
    - In a large mixing bowl, whisk together the flour, baking powder, baking soda, and salt.
    - Add the cold butter cubes to the flour mixture. Using a pastry cutter or your fingertips, cut the butter into the flour until the mixture resembles coarse crumbs.
3. Add Cheese and Herbs:
    - Stir in the grated cheddar cheese and chopped fresh herbs until evenly distributed.
4. Combine Wet Ingredients:
    - In a separate bowl, whisk together the Greek yogurt (or sour cream) and milk until smooth.
5. Form the Dough:
    - Make a well in the center of the dry ingredients. Pour the yogurt-milk mixture into the well.
    - Using a fork or spatula, gently mix until the dough comes together. Be careful not to overmix.
6. Shape the Scones:
    - Turn the dough out onto a lightly floured surface. Pat the dough into a circle or rectangle about 1 inch thick.
7. Cut the Scones:
    - Using a sharp knife or a biscuit cutter, cut the dough into scones of desired shape and size. For traditional triangular scones, cut the circle into wedges.
8. Bake the Scones:

- Place the scones on the prepared baking sheet, leaving a little space between each one.
- Brush the tops of the scones with beaten egg wash. Optionally, sprinkle additional grated cheese and herbs on top for extra flavor and appearance.

9. Bake:
   - Bake in the preheated oven for 15-18 minutes, or until the scones are golden brown on top and cooked through. They should sound hollow when tapped on the bottom.
10. Cool and Serve:
    - Transfer the cheese and herb scones to a wire rack to cool slightly before serving.
    - Serve warm or at room temperature. Enjoy them plain or with butter, cream cheese, or your favorite spread.

Tips:

- **Cheese Variation:** Experiment with different cheeses such as Gruyère, mozzarella, or a combination of cheeses for different flavors.
- **Herb Options:** Customize the scones with your favorite herbs like rosemary, dill, basil, or a blend of herbs for added freshness.
- **Storage:** Store leftover scones in an airtight container at room temperature for up to 2 days. Reheat briefly in the oven or toaster oven before serving.

These cheese and herb scones are buttery, cheesy, and bursting with savory flavors from the herbs. They make a wonderful addition to any meal or as a tasty snack on their own!

Cheese and Spinach Quiche

Ingredients:

For the Pastry Crust:

- 1 1/4 cups all-purpose flour
- 1/2 teaspoon salt
- 1/2 cup cold unsalted butter, cut into small cubes
- 3-4 tablespoons ice water

For the Filling:

- 1 tablespoon olive oil
- 1 small onion, finely chopped
- 2 cloves garlic, minced
- 4 cups fresh spinach leaves, chopped
- 1 cup shredded cheese (such as Gruyère, Swiss, cheddar, or a combination)
- 4 large eggs
- 1 cup milk (whole milk or half-and-half)
- Salt and pepper, to taste
- Pinch of nutmeg (optional)

Instructions:

1. Make the Pastry Crust:
    - In a large bowl, whisk together the flour and salt.
    - Add the cold butter cubes to the flour mixture. Use a pastry cutter or your fingertips to quickly work the butter into the flour until the mixture resembles coarse crumbs.
    - Gradually add the ice water, 1 tablespoon at a time, mixing with a fork until the dough just begins to come together.
    - Turn the dough out onto a lightly floured surface and knead gently until it forms a cohesive ball. Flatten into a disk, wrap in plastic wrap, and refrigerate for at least 30 minutes.
2. Prepare the Filling:
    - Preheat your oven to 375°F (190°C).
    - In a large skillet, heat olive oil over medium heat. Add chopped onion and sauté until softened, about 3-4 minutes.
    - Add minced garlic and cook for another 1 minute until fragrant.
    - Add chopped spinach to the skillet and cook until wilted, about 2-3 minutes. Remove from heat and let cool slightly.
3. Assemble the Quiche:
    - On a lightly floured surface, roll out the chilled pastry dough into a circle large enough to fit into a 9-inch quiche or pie dish. Transfer the dough to the dish and

press it gently into the bottom and sides. Trim any excess dough and crimp the edges.
    - Sprinkle shredded cheese evenly over the bottom of the pastry crust.
    - In a bowl, whisk together eggs and milk until well combined. Season with salt, pepper, and a pinch of nutmeg if using.
    - Spread the spinach mixture evenly over the cheese in the pastry crust.
4. Bake the Quiche:
    - Carefully pour the egg mixture over the spinach and cheese in the crust.
    - Place the quiche on a baking sheet (to catch any spills) and bake in the preheated oven for 35-40 minutes, or until the quiche is set in the center and the crust is golden brown.
5. Cool and Serve:
    - Remove the quiche from the oven and let it cool for 10 minutes before slicing and serving.
    - Serve warm or at room temperature. Enjoy this delicious cheese and spinach quiche as a main dish for brunch or a light dinner.

Tips:

- Variations: Feel free to add other ingredients such as cooked bacon, mushrooms, or sun-dried tomatoes to customize your quiche.
- Make-Ahead: You can prepare the pastry dough and filling ahead of time. Assemble the quiche and refrigerate, covered, until ready to bake.
- Storage: Leftover quiche can be stored in the refrigerator for up to 3 days. Reheat gently in the oven or microwave before serving.

This cheese and spinach quiche is flavorful, creamy, and perfect for any occasion. It's a versatile dish that can be enjoyed hot or cold, making it a great option for brunch gatherings or a satisfying meal at home.

Cheesy Grits

Ingredients:

- 1 cup quick-cooking grits (not instant)
- 4 cups water
- 1 teaspoon salt
- 1 cup shredded cheese (such as cheddar, Gruyère, or a blend)
- 2 tablespoons unsalted butter
- 1/4 cup heavy cream (optional, for extra creaminess)
- Salt and pepper, to taste

Instructions:

1. Cook the Grits:
   - In a medium saucepan, bring 4 cups of water to a boil.
   - Stir in the grits and salt. Reduce the heat to low and simmer, stirring occasionally, until the grits are thickened and tender, about 10-15 minutes. Stir more frequently towards the end of cooking to prevent sticking.
2. Add Cheese and Butter:
   - Once the grits are cooked and creamy, remove the saucepan from the heat.
   - Stir in the shredded cheese and unsalted butter until melted and well combined.
3. Adjust Consistency:
   - If desired, stir in the heavy cream to achieve a creamier texture.
   - Season with salt and pepper to taste.
4. Serve:
   - Serve the cheesy grits immediately while hot.
   - Optionally, garnish with additional shredded cheese or chopped fresh herbs before serving.

Tips:

- Grits Texture: Adjust the amount of water or cooking time based on the desired consistency of the grits. For creamier grits, you can use milk instead of water or add more butter and cheese.
- Cheese Variation: Experiment with different types of cheese to vary the flavor. Sharp cheddar adds a tangy kick, while Gruyère lends a nutty richness.
- Customization: Add cooked bacon bits, sautéed vegetables (like spinach or bell peppers), or diced jalapeños for additional flavor and texture.

Cheesy grits are versatile and can be served as a side dish for breakfast, brunch, or dinner. They pair well with eggs, bacon, sausage, or as a comforting base for sautéed shrimp or grilled chicken. Enjoy this Southern classic dish that's sure to please everyone at the table!

Cheese and Sausage Breakfast Casserole

Ingredients:

- 1 pound breakfast sausage (pork or turkey), casings removed
- 1 small onion, finely chopped
- 1 red bell pepper, diced
- 6 cups cubed bread (French bread or sourdough work well)
- 2 cups shredded cheese (such as cheddar, Monterey Jack, or a blend)
- 8 large eggs
- 2 cups milk (whole milk or half-and-half)
- 1 teaspoon Dijon mustard
- 1/2 teaspoon salt
- 1/4 teaspoon black pepper
- 1/4 teaspoon paprika
- Fresh parsley or chives, chopped (for garnish, optional)

Instructions:

1. Preheat Oven:
    - Preheat your oven to 350°F (175°C). Grease a 9x13 inch baking dish with butter or cooking spray.
2. Cook the Sausage and Vegetables:
    - In a large skillet, cook the breakfast sausage over medium-high heat, breaking it up into crumbles with a spatula, until browned and cooked through.
    - Add chopped onion and diced red bell pepper to the skillet. Cook for 3-4 minutes, until vegetables are softened. Remove from heat and set aside.
3. Assemble the Casserole:
    - Spread half of the cubed bread evenly in the prepared baking dish.
    - Sprinkle half of the shredded cheese over the bread.
    - Spread the cooked sausage and vegetable mixture evenly over the cheese and bread layer.
    - Top with the remaining cubed bread and shredded cheese.
4. Prepare the Egg Mixture:
    - In a large bowl, whisk together eggs, milk, Dijon mustard, salt, pepper, and paprika until well combined.
5. Pour and Bake:
    - Pour the egg mixture evenly over the bread, sausage, and cheese layers in the baking dish.
    - Gently press down on the bread cubes to ensure they are soaked in the egg mixture.
    - Cover the baking dish with foil and let it sit at room temperature for 15-20 minutes to allow the bread to absorb the egg mixture.
6. Bake the Casserole:

- Bake the casserole, covered with foil, in the preheated oven for 40-45 minutes.
- Remove the foil and bake for an additional 10-15 minutes, or until the top is golden brown and the center is set.

7. Cool and Serve:
    - Remove the breakfast casserole from the oven and let it cool for 5-10 minutes before slicing.
    - Garnish with chopped fresh parsley or chives if desired.
    - Serve warm, cut into squares, and enjoy!

Tips:

- **Variations:** Customize the casserole by adding diced tomatoes, spinach, mushrooms, or your favorite herbs.
- **Make-Ahead:** You can assemble the casserole the night before, cover, and refrigerate. In the morning, bake as directed, adding a few extra minutes of baking time if needed.
- **Storage:** Leftover breakfast casserole can be stored in the refrigerator for up to 3 days. Reheat individual servings in the microwave or oven.

This cheese and sausage breakfast casserole is a comforting and satisfying dish that's perfect for a weekend brunch or holiday gathering. It's sure to become a favorite with its layers of savory sausage, cheese, and fluffy eggs baked into a delicious breakfast treat!

Cheese Ravioli

Ingredients:

For the Pasta Dough:

- 2 cups all-purpose flour, plus extra for dusting
- 3 large eggs
- 1 tablespoon olive oil
- Pinch of salt

For the Cheese Filling:

- 1 cup ricotta cheese
- 1/2 cup grated Parmesan cheese
- 1 egg yolk
- 1 tablespoon chopped fresh parsley
- Salt and pepper, to taste
- Optional: pinch of nutmeg

For the Tomato Sauce:

- 2 tablespoons olive oil
- 2 cloves garlic, minced
- 1 can (14 oz) crushed tomatoes
- 1/2 teaspoon dried oregano
- Salt and pepper, to taste
- Fresh basil leaves, chopped (for garnish)

Instructions:

Step 1: Make the Pasta Dough

1. On a clean work surface, mound the flour and make a well in the center.
2. Add the eggs, olive oil, and salt to the well.
3. Using a fork, gradually whisk the eggs, gradually incorporating the flour from the edges of the well until a dough forms.
4. Knead the dough for about 10 minutes until smooth and elastic. Cover with plastic wrap and let rest for 30 minutes.

Step 2: Prepare the Cheese Filling

1. In a bowl, combine the ricotta cheese, grated Parmesan cheese, egg yolk, chopped parsley, salt, pepper, and nutmeg (if using). Mix well until smooth and evenly combined.

Step 3: Roll Out and Fill the Ravioli

1. Divide the pasta dough into 4 equal portions.
2. Working with one portion at a time, flatten it into a rough rectangle shape.
3. Use a pasta machine or rolling pin to roll out the dough thinly, about 1/16 inch thick. Dust with flour as needed to prevent sticking.
4. Place teaspoonfuls of the cheese filling about 1 inch apart on one sheet of pasta dough.
5. Brush the dough around the filling with water to moisten.
6. Top with another sheet of pasta dough. Press gently around each mound of filling to seal and remove any air bubbles.
7. Use a sharp knife or a fluted pastry wheel to cut out individual ravioli squares or circles.

Step 4: Cook the Ravioli

1. Bring a large pot of salted water to a boil.
2. Carefully add the ravioli and cook for about 3-4 minutes, or until they float to the surface and are tender.
3. Remove the ravioli with a slotted spoon and transfer to a plate.

Step 5: Make the Tomato Sauce

1. In a large skillet, heat olive oil over medium heat. Add minced garlic and cook until fragrant, about 1 minute.
2. Stir in crushed tomatoes and dried oregano. Season with salt and pepper to taste. Simmer for 5-7 minutes, stirring occasionally, until the sauce thickens slightly.

Step 6: Serve

1. Divide the cooked ravioli among serving plates. Spoon the tomato sauce over the ravioli.
2. Garnish with chopped fresh basil leaves and additional grated Parmesan cheese if desired. Serve immediately.

Tips:

- Variations: You can add spinach or herbs like basil or thyme to the cheese filling for extra flavor.
- Freezing: If you have leftover uncooked ravioli, you can freeze them on a baking sheet until firm, then transfer to a freezer bag. Cook from frozen, adding a couple of extra minutes to the cooking time.
- Homemade Sauce: If you prefer a creamier sauce, you can replace the tomato sauce with a simple butter and sage sauce or a creamy Alfredo sauce.

Enjoy these homemade cheese ravioli with tomato sauce for a comforting and delicious Italian-inspired meal!

Mozzarella Sticks

Ingredients:

- 12 mozzarella string cheese sticks
- 1 cup all-purpose flour
- 2 large eggs, beaten
- 1 cup breadcrumbs (plain or seasoned)
- 1/2 cup grated Parmesan cheese
- 1/2 teaspoon garlic powder
- 1/2 teaspoon dried oregano
- 1/2 teaspoon dried basil
- Salt and pepper, to taste
- Oil for frying (vegetable oil or canola oil)

Instructions:

1. Prepare the Breading Station:
    - Set up three shallow bowls or plates. Place the flour in the first bowl, beaten eggs in the second bowl, and breadcrumbs mixed with grated Parmesan cheese, garlic powder, dried oregano, dried basil, salt, and pepper in the third bowl.
2. Prepare the Mozzarella Sticks:
    - Remove the mozzarella sticks from their packaging and cut them in half to make shorter sticks, if desired.
3. Coat the Mozzarella Sticks:
    - One at a time, coat each mozzarella stick in the flour, shaking off any excess.
    - Dip the flour-coated stick into the beaten eggs, ensuring it is evenly coated.
    - Roll the egg-coated stick in the breadcrumb mixture, pressing gently to adhere the breadcrumbs to the cheese.
4. Repeat Coating (Optional):
    - For a thicker coating, you can repeat the process of dipping the sticks in the egg and breadcrumb mixture.
5. Chill the Mozzarella Sticks (Optional):
    - Place the coated mozzarella sticks on a baking sheet lined with parchment paper and chill in the refrigerator for 20-30 minutes. This helps the breading adhere better during frying.
6. Fry the Mozzarella Sticks:
    - In a large skillet or pot, heat enough oil to submerge the mozzarella sticks to 350°F (175°C) over medium-high heat.
    - Carefully add a few mozzarella sticks to the hot oil, making sure not to overcrowd the pan. Fry for 1-2 minutes, or until golden brown and crispy.
    - Remove the fried mozzarella sticks with a slotted spoon and transfer to a plate lined with paper towels to drain excess oil. Repeat with the remaining mozzarella sticks.

7. Serve:
    - Serve the crispy mozzarella sticks hot, with marinara sauce or your favorite dipping sauce on the side.

Tips:

- Cheese Variations: Experiment with different types of cheese like cheddar or pepper jack for a twist on traditional mozzarella sticks.
- Baking Option: If you prefer a healthier alternative, you can bake the coated mozzarella sticks in a preheated oven at 400°F (200°C) for 8-10 minutes until golden brown and crispy.
- Freezing: To freeze mozzarella sticks for later use, arrange the breaded sticks in a single layer on a baking sheet and freeze until solid. Once frozen, transfer them to a freezer bag. Fry or bake from frozen, adding a few extra minutes to the cooking time.

Enjoy these homemade mozzarella sticks as a delicious snack or appetizer, perfect for parties, game nights, or any occasion!

Cheese-Stuffed Meatloaf

Ingredients:

For the Meatloaf:

- 2 pounds ground beef (or a mix of beef and pork)
- 1 cup breadcrumbs
- 1/2 cup milk
- 2 eggs, beaten
- 1 small onion, finely chopped
- 2 cloves garlic, minced
- 1/4 cup ketchup
- 1 tablespoon Worcestershire sauce
- 1 teaspoon dried oregano
- 1 teaspoon dried thyme
- Salt and pepper, to taste

For the Cheese Filling:

- 8 ounces mozzarella cheese (or any cheese you prefer), cut into sticks or shredded

For the Glaze:

- 1/2 cup ketchup
- 2 tablespoons brown sugar
- 1 tablespoon Dijon mustard

Instructions:

1. Preheat Oven:
   - Preheat your oven to 350°F (175°C). Line a baking sheet with parchment paper or foil.
2. Prepare the Meatloaf Mixture:
   - In a large bowl, combine the ground beef, breadcrumbs, milk, beaten eggs, chopped onion, minced garlic, ketchup, Worcestershire sauce, dried oregano, dried thyme, salt, and pepper. Mix until well combined.
3. Shape the Meatloaf:
   - Divide the meatloaf mixture into two equal portions.
   - Take one portion and press it into a rectangle or oval shape on the prepared baking sheet, about 1/2 inch thick.
4. Add the Cheese Filling:
   - Arrange the mozzarella cheese sticks or shredded cheese down the center of the meatloaf, leaving a border around the edges.
5. Form the Meatloaf:

- Take the remaining portion of the meatloaf mixture and press it evenly over the cheese filling, sealing the edges well to enclose the cheese.
6. Prepare the Glaze:
    - In a small bowl, whisk together the ketchup, brown sugar, and Dijon mustard until smooth.
7. Glaze and Bake:
    - Brush the glaze over the top and sides of the meatloaf.
    - Bake in the preheated oven for 50-60 minutes, or until the meatloaf is cooked through and the internal temperature reaches 160°F (70°C).
8. Rest and Serve:
    - Remove the meatloaf from the oven and let it rest for 10 minutes before slicing.
    - Slice the cheese-stuffed meatloaf and serve warm, garnished with fresh herbs if desired.

Tips:

- Cheese Variation: Experiment with different cheeses like cheddar, provolone, or pepper jack for different flavors.
- Additions: You can add finely chopped bell peppers, mushrooms, or herbs like parsley or basil to the meatloaf mixture for added texture and flavor.
- Serving Suggestions: Serve the cheese-stuffed meatloaf with mashed potatoes, steamed vegetables, or a side salad for a complete meal.

This cheese-stuffed meatloaf recipe is sure to be a hit with its cheesy surprise inside moist and flavorful meatloaf. It's a comforting dish that's perfect for family dinners or special occasions!

Cheese and Herb Biscuits

Ingredients:

- 2 cups all-purpose flour
- 1 tablespoon baking powder
- 1/2 teaspoon baking soda
- 1/2 teaspoon salt
- 1/2 cup cold unsalted butter, cut into small cubes
- 1 cup shredded cheese (cheddar, Gruyère, or your favorite melting cheese)
- 2 tablespoons chopped fresh herbs (such as parsley, chives, thyme, or a combination)
- 3/4 cup buttermilk (or substitute with 3/4 cup milk mixed with 1 tablespoon lemon juice or white vinegar)

Instructions:

1. Preheat Oven and Prepare Baking Sheet:
    - Preheat your oven to 425°F (220°C). Line a baking sheet with parchment paper or lightly grease it.
2. Mix Dry Ingredients:
    - In a large bowl, whisk together the flour, baking powder, baking soda, and salt.
3. Cut in Butter:
    - Add the cold butter cubes to the flour mixture. Using a pastry cutter or your fingertips, cut the butter into the flour until the mixture resembles coarse crumbs.
4. Add Cheese and Herbs:
    - Stir in the shredded cheese and chopped fresh herbs until evenly distributed.
5. Combine Wet Ingredients:
    - Make a well in the center of the dry ingredients. Pour in the buttermilk (or milk mixture).
6. Form the Dough:
    - Stir the mixture with a fork or wooden spoon until the dough begins to come together. It will be slightly sticky.
7. Shape and Cut Biscuits:
    - Turn the dough out onto a lightly floured surface. Pat it into a rectangle about 1/2 inch thick.
    - Use a floured biscuit cutter or a sharp knife to cut out biscuits. Press straight down without twisting to ensure even rising.
8. Bake the Biscuits:
    - Place the biscuits on the prepared baking sheet, leaving a little space between each one.
    - Bake in the preheated oven for 12-15 minutes, or until the biscuits are golden brown on top and cooked through.
9. Cool and Serve:

- Remove the biscuits from the oven and let them cool on a wire rack for a few minutes before serving.

Tips:

- Cheese Variation: Experiment with different types of cheese like Gruyère, mozzarella, or a blend of cheeses for different flavors.
- Herb Options: Customize the biscuits with your favorite herbs such as rosemary, dill, basil, or a combination of herbs for added freshness.
- Storage: Store leftover biscuits in an airtight container at room temperature for up to 2 days. Reheat briefly in the oven or toaster oven before serving.

These cheese and herb biscuits are buttery, flaky, and bursting with savory flavors from the cheese and herbs. They are perfect for breakfast, brunch, or as a tasty side dish with meals. Enjoy them warm with a pat of butter or alongside your favorite soup or salad!

Cheese-Topped French Onion Soup

Ingredients:

- 4 large yellow onions, thinly sliced
- 3 tablespoons unsalted butter
- 2 tablespoons olive oil
- 1 teaspoon granulated sugar (optional, to aid in caramelization)
- 2 cloves garlic, minced
- 1/2 cup dry white wine (optional)
- 6 cups beef broth (or vegetable broth for a vegetarian version)
- 2 bay leaves
- 1 teaspoon fresh thyme leaves (or 1/2 teaspoon dried thyme)
- Salt and pepper, to taste
- Baguette slices (about 1-inch thick), toasted
- 1 1/2 cups shredded Gruyère cheese (or Swiss cheese, or a combination)

Instructions:

1. Caramelize the Onions:
    - In a large pot or Dutch oven, melt the butter and olive oil over medium heat.
    - Add the sliced onions and cook, stirring occasionally, until they become very soft and golden brown, about 30-40 minutes.
    - If using, sprinkle the sugar over the onions to aid in caramelization. Stir occasionally to prevent burning.
2. Add Garlic and Deglaze:
    - Add minced garlic to the caramelized onions and cook for 1-2 minutes until fragrant.
    - If using, pour in the white wine to deglaze the pot, scraping up any browned bits from the bottom.
3. Simmer the Soup:
    - Pour in the beef broth and add the bay leaves and thyme. Season with salt and pepper to taste.
    - Bring the soup to a simmer over medium-low heat. Cover and cook for 20-30 minutes to allow the flavors to meld together.
4. Prepare the Baguette Slices:
    - Meanwhile, preheat your oven's broiler.
    - Arrange the toasted baguette slices on a baking sheet lined with parchment paper.
5. Assemble the Soup:
    - Remove the bay leaves from the soup and discard.
    - Ladle the hot soup into oven-safe bowls or crocks.
    - Place a few slices of toasted baguette on top of each bowl of soup, covering the surface.

- Sprinkle a generous amount of shredded Gruyère cheese over the bread slices, covering them completely.
6. Broil Until Cheese is Melted and Golden:
    - Place the soup bowls under the broiler and broil for 2-3 minutes, or until the cheese is melted and bubbly, and starting to brown on top.
7. Serve:
    - Carefully remove the soup bowls from the oven (they will be hot!).
    - Garnish with additional fresh thyme leaves if desired.
    - Serve immediately, ensuring each serving has a piece of cheesy baguette to enjoy with the soup.

Tips:

- Onion Caramelization: Take your time caramelizing the onions over low heat to develop deep flavor and sweetness.
- Cheese Variation: Experiment with different cheeses like Swiss, provolone, or mozzarella for different flavor profiles.
- Make-Ahead: You can prepare the soup base and caramelize the onions ahead of time. Assemble and broil the cheese-topped soup just before serving.

This cheese-topped French onion soup is a comforting and satisfying dish, perfect for a cozy meal on a chilly day. The combination of caramelized onions, flavorful broth, crusty baguette, and gooey melted cheese makes it a timeless favorite. Enjoy this homemade version with its rich flavors and cheesy goodness!

Cheese-Stuffed Zucchini Boats

Ingredients:

- 4 medium zucchini
- 1 tablespoon olive oil
- 1 small onion, finely chopped
- 2 cloves garlic, minced
- 1 cup ricotta cheese
- 1/2 cup grated Parmesan cheese, plus extra for topping
- 1 cup shredded mozzarella cheese
- 1/4 cup chopped fresh basil or parsley
- Salt and pepper, to taste
- Optional: Red pepper flakes or Italian seasoning, for added flavor

Instructions:

1. Preheat Oven:
    - Preheat your oven to 400°F (200°C). Grease a baking dish large enough to hold the zucchini boats.
2. Prepare the Zucchini:
    - Wash the zucchini and trim off the ends. Cut each zucchini in half lengthwise.
    - Use a spoon to scoop out the center flesh of each zucchini half, leaving about 1/4-inch thick shells. Reserve the scooped-out flesh for later use.
3. Prepare the Filling:
    - In a skillet, heat olive oil over medium heat. Add chopped onion and cook until softened, about 5 minutes.
    - Add minced garlic and cook for another 1-2 minutes until fragrant. Remove from heat and let cool slightly.
4. Make the Cheese Mixture:
    - In a bowl, combine ricotta cheese, grated Parmesan cheese, shredded mozzarella cheese, chopped basil or parsley, and the cooled onion and garlic mixture.
    - Season with salt, pepper, and optional red pepper flakes or Italian seasoning to taste. Mix until well combined.
5. Fill the Zucchini Boats:
    - Spoon the cheese mixture evenly into the hollowed-out zucchini halves, pressing gently to fill.
    - Place the filled zucchini boats in the prepared baking dish.
6. Bake:
    - Sprinkle additional grated Parmesan cheese on top of each stuffed zucchini boat.
    - Cover the baking dish with foil and bake in the preheated oven for 20-25 minutes.
7. Broil (Optional):

- Remove the foil and broil the stuffed zucchini boats for an additional 2-3 minutes, or until the cheese is golden and bubbly.

8. Serve:
    - Remove from the oven and let cool slightly before serving.
    - Garnish with additional chopped herbs if desired.

Tips:

- Variations: Add cooked crumbled bacon, diced tomatoes, or spinach to the cheese mixture for added flavor and texture.
- Make-Ahead: You can prepare the zucchini boats and cheese filling ahead of time and assemble just before baking.
- Serving Suggestions: Serve cheese-stuffed zucchini boats as a side dish or light main course, accompanied by a salad or crusty bread.

Enjoy these cheese-stuffed zucchini boats as a tasty and satisfying dish that's perfect for a family meal or entertaining guests. The combination of creamy cheeses and fresh zucchini makes it a delicious and healthy option!

Cheese and Apple Platter

Ingredients:

- Assorted cheeses (choose a variety such as cheddar, Gouda, Brie, blue cheese, and/or goat cheese)
- 2-3 different types of apples (such as Granny Smith, Honeycrisp, or Fuji)
- Crackers or bread slices
- Honey, for drizzling (optional)
- Nuts (such as almonds or walnuts, optional)
- Fresh herbs (such as rosemary sprigs, for garnish)

Instructions:

1. Select and Arrange Cheeses:
   - Choose a selection of cheeses with different textures and flavors. Arrange them on a large serving platter or wooden board, leaving space between each type of cheese.
2. Prepare the Apples:
   - Wash and dry the apples. Core them and slice them thinly or into wedges. Arrange the apple slices around the cheeses on the platter.
3. Add Crackers or Bread:
   - Place a variety of crackers or bread slices next to the cheeses and apples. Choose different types such as water crackers, whole grain crackers, or baguette slices.
4. Optional Garnishes:
   - Drizzle honey over the cheeses or serve it in a small bowl on the platter for dipping.
   - Scatter nuts (like almonds or walnuts) around the platter for added crunch and texture.
   - Garnish with fresh herbs, such as rosemary sprigs, for a decorative touch and added aroma.
5. Serve and Enjoy:
   - Place the cheese and apple platter on the table and invite guests to help themselves.
   - Encourage guests to mix and match cheeses with different types of apples and crackers, and to explore different flavor combinations.

Tips:

- Cheese Selection: Include a mix of soft cheeses (like Brie or goat cheese), semi-hard cheeses (like Gouda or cheddar), and blue cheeses for variety in flavor and texture.
- Apple Variety: Choose apples that complement the cheeses, balancing their sweetness and tartness.

- Presentation: Arrange the cheeses, apples, and accompaniments in an aesthetically pleasing manner on the platter or board.
- Pairings: Offer wine or sparkling cider as beverages to complement the flavors of the cheese and apple platter.

This cheese and apple platter makes for a wonderful appetizer or snack, perfect for gatherings, parties, or even a cozy night in. It's a versatile and crowd-pleasing dish that combines the best of sweet and savory flavors!

Cheesy Cauliflower Bake

Ingredients:

- 1 large head of cauliflower, cut into florets
- 2 tablespoons unsalted butter
- 2 tablespoons all-purpose flour
- 1 1/2 cups milk (whole milk or 2%)
- 1 cup shredded cheddar cheese
- 1/2 cup shredded mozzarella cheese
- 1/4 cup grated Parmesan cheese
- 1 teaspoon Dijon mustard (optional)
- 1/2 teaspoon garlic powder
- Salt and pepper, to taste
- 1/4 cup breadcrumbs (optional, for topping)
- Fresh parsley, chopped (for garnish)

Instructions:

1. Preheat Oven:
    - Preheat your oven to 375°F (190°C). Grease a 9x13-inch baking dish with butter or cooking spray.
2. Steam the Cauliflower:
    - Place the cauliflower florets in a steamer basket over boiling water. Steam for about 5-7 minutes, or until the cauliflower is tender-crisp. Drain well and set aside.
3. Make the Cheese Sauce:
    - In a medium saucepan, melt the butter over medium heat. Add the flour and whisk constantly for 1-2 minutes to make a roux.
    - Gradually pour in the milk, whisking constantly to prevent lumps.
    - Cook the sauce until it thickens and bubbles, about 3-5 minutes.
    - Reduce heat to low. Stir in the shredded cheddar cheese, mozzarella cheese, and grated Parmesan cheese until melted and smooth.
    - Add Dijon mustard (if using), garlic powder, salt, and pepper to taste. Stir until well combined.
4. Combine Cauliflower and Cheese Sauce:
    - Place the steamed cauliflower florets into the prepared baking dish.
    - Pour the cheese sauce over the cauliflower, spreading evenly to coat all pieces.
5. Bake the Cauliflower Bake:
    - If using breadcrumbs, sprinkle them evenly over the top of the cauliflower bake.
    - Bake in the preheated oven for 25-30 minutes, or until the top is golden brown and bubbly.
6. Serve:
    - Remove from the oven and let cool for a few minutes before serving.

- Garnish with chopped fresh parsley before serving.

Tips:

- Variations: Add cooked bacon or diced ham for extra flavor and protein.
- Vegetarian Option: Use vegetable broth instead of chicken broth.
- Make-Ahead: Assemble the dish up to a day ahead of time, cover tightly, and refrigerate until ready to bake. Increase baking time slightly if baking straight from the refrigerator.

This cheesy cauliflower bake is creamy, flavorful, and makes a delicious side dish or even a vegetarian main course. It's perfect for family dinners, holidays, or potluck gatherings, offering a comforting and satisfying dish that everyone will enjoy!

Cheese-Stuffed Soft Pretzels

Ingredients:

For the Pretzel Dough:

- 1 1/2 cups warm water (110°F to 115°F)
- 1 tablespoon granulated sugar
- 2 teaspoons kosher salt
- 1 packet (2 1/4 teaspoons) active dry yeast
- 4 1/2 cups all-purpose flour
- 4 tablespoons unsalted butter, melted
- Vegetable oil, for greasing the bowl

For the Cheese Filling:

- 8 ounces block of cheddar cheese or mozzarella cheese, cut into sticks (about 3-4 inches long and 1/2 inch wide)

For Boiling:

- 10 cups water
- 2/3 cup baking soda

For Topping:

- 1 large egg yolk beaten with 1 tablespoon water, for egg wash
- Pretzel salt or coarse sea salt, for sprinkling

Instructions:

1. Make the Pretzel Dough:
    - In the bowl of a stand mixer fitted with the dough hook attachment, combine the warm water, sugar, and salt. Sprinkle the yeast on top and let it sit for 5 minutes until foamy.
    - Add the flour and melted butter to the yeast mixture. Mix on low speed until the dough comes together. Increase the speed to medium and knead until the dough is smooth and elastic, about 5 minutes.
    - Remove the dough from the bowl and place it in a greased bowl. Cover with plastic wrap and let it rise in a warm place until doubled in size, about 1 hour.
2. Prepare the Cheese Filling:
    - While the dough is rising, prepare the cheese filling. Cut the block of cheese into sticks.
3. Shape the Pretzels:

- Preheat your oven to 450°F (230°C). Line two baking sheets with parchment paper and lightly grease them with oil.
- Punch down the risen dough and divide it into 8 equal pieces. Roll each piece into a long rope, about 24 inches long.
- Flatten each rope with your hands or a rolling pin. Place a cheese stick in the center and fold the dough over the cheese, pinching the edges to seal and encase the cheese completely. Roll the filled dough gently to form a uniform rope again.
- Shape each filled rope into a pretzel shape: form a U-shape, then cross the ends over each other and press them onto the bottom of the U to form the classic pretzel shape.

4. Boil the Pretzels:
    - In a large pot, bring the water and baking soda to a boil. Working one or two at a time, carefully place the pretzels into the boiling water for 30 seconds. Use a slotted spoon to remove them and place them back onto the prepared baking sheets.
5. Bake the Pretzels:
    - Brush each pretzel with the egg wash and sprinkle with pretzel salt or coarse sea salt.
    - Bake in the preheated oven for 12-15 minutes, or until golden brown and cooked through.
6. Serve:
    - Remove the pretzels from the oven and let them cool on a wire rack for a few minutes before serving.

Tips:

- Cheese Variations: Experiment with different cheeses like pepper jack, Swiss, or provolone for different flavors.
- Serve with Dips: Enjoy these cheese-stuffed pretzels warm, either on their own or with mustard, cheese sauce, or marinara sauce for dipping.
- Storage: Store leftover pretzels in an airtight container at room temperature for up to 2 days. Reheat in a toaster oven or microwave before serving.

These cheese-stuffed soft pretzels are a delicious homemade snack or appetizer that's sure to be a hit. They combine the classic soft pretzel texture with the gooey goodness of melted cheese inside, making them perfect for any occasion!

Cheesy Nachos

Ingredients:

- 1 bag (about 10-12 ounces) tortilla chips (choose your favorite variety)
- 2 cups shredded cheese (cheddar, Monterey Jack, or a blend)
- 1 cup cooked black beans or refried beans
- 1 cup diced tomatoes
- 1/2 cup sliced jalapeños (optional, for heat)
- 1/4 cup sliced black olives
- 1/4 cup chopped green onions or cilantro, for garnish
- Sour cream, guacamole, salsa, or your favorite nacho toppings

Instructions:

1. Preheat Oven:
    - Preheat your oven to 375°F (190°C). Line a large baking sheet with parchment paper or aluminum foil.
2. Layer the Chips:
    - Arrange the tortilla chips in a single layer on the prepared baking sheet, overlapping slightly if needed.
3. Add Cheese and Toppings:
    - Sprinkle the shredded cheese evenly over the tortilla chips, ensuring each chip gets some cheese. Use more or less cheese according to your preference.
4. Add Additional Toppings:
    - Distribute the cooked black beans or refried beans, diced tomatoes, sliced jalapeños (if using), and black olives evenly over the cheese-topped chips.
5. Bake in the Oven:
    - Place the baking sheet in the preheated oven and bake for 8-10 minutes, or until the cheese is melted and bubbly.
6. Garnish and Serve:
    - Remove the nachos from the oven and immediately sprinkle chopped green onions or cilantro over the top.
    - Serve the cheesy nachos hot with sour cream, guacamole, salsa, or your favorite toppings on the side.

Tips:

- Variations: Customize your nachos with additional toppings like cooked ground beef or shredded chicken, diced onions, bell peppers, or corn.
- Cheese Options: Experiment with different cheeses or cheese blends for varied flavors. Pepper jack cheese adds a spicy kick, while mozzarella can give a stringy, gooey texture.

- Serve Immediately: Nachos are best served immediately after baking to ensure the chips stay crispy and the cheese remains melted and gooey.

Cheesy nachos are a crowd-pleasing snack that's perfect for parties, game nights, or casual gatherings. They are versatile and easy to customize with your favorite toppings, making them a favorite for both kids and adults alike!

Cheese and Broccoli Soup

Ingredients:

- 4 tablespoons unsalted butter
- 1 small onion, chopped
- 2 cloves garlic, minced
- 1/4 cup all-purpose flour
- 3 cups vegetable or chicken broth
- 2 cups milk (whole milk or 2%)
- 1/2 teaspoon dried thyme (or 1 teaspoon fresh thyme leaves)
- 1/2 teaspoon dried oregano
- Salt and pepper, to taste
- 3 cups broccoli florets, chopped into small pieces
- 2 cups shredded cheddar cheese
- 1 cup shredded mozzarella cheese (optional, for extra creaminess)
- 1/2 cup grated Parmesan cheese
- Optional garnish: Additional shredded cheese, chopped fresh parsley or chives

Instructions:

1. Sauté Onion and Garlic:
    - In a large pot or Dutch oven, melt the butter over medium heat. Add the chopped onion and cook until softened, about 5-7 minutes. Add minced garlic and cook for an additional 1-2 minutes until fragrant.
2. Make Roux:
    - Sprinkle the flour over the onion and garlic mixture. Stir constantly for 1-2 minutes to cook the flour and form a roux.
3. Add Broth and Milk:
    - Gradually pour in the vegetable or chicken broth, stirring constantly to incorporate the roux into the liquid.
    - Stir in the milk, dried thyme, dried oregano, salt, and pepper. Bring the mixture to a simmer, stirring occasionally.
4. Cook Broccoli:
    - Add the chopped broccoli florets to the pot. Simmer for 10-12 minutes, or until the broccoli is tender and cooked through.
5. Blend Soup (Optional):
    - For a smoother texture, you can use an immersion blender to blend part of the soup directly in the pot. Alternatively, transfer a portion of the soup to a blender and blend until smooth, then return it to the pot.
6. Add Cheese:
    - Reduce heat to low. Gradually stir in the shredded cheddar cheese, mozzarella cheese (if using), and grated Parmesan cheese until melted and smooth. Adjust seasoning with salt and pepper as needed.

7. Serve:
   - Ladle the cheese and broccoli soup into bowls. Garnish with additional shredded cheese and chopped fresh parsley or chives if desired.

Tips:

- Vegetable Variation: Add diced carrots or cauliflower along with the broccoli for additional flavor and texture.
- Creamy Texture: For an even creamier soup, add a splash of heavy cream or half-and-half before serving.
- Storage: Store leftover soup in an airtight container in the refrigerator for up to 3 days. Reheat gently on the stove, adding a splash of milk or broth to thin if needed.

This cheese and broccoli soup is hearty, flavorful, and perfect for chilly days. It pairs wonderfully with crusty bread or a side salad for a satisfying meal. Enjoy the creamy goodness of cheese and the wholesome taste of broccoli in every spoonful!

Cheese and Chive Scones

Ingredients:

- 2 cups all-purpose flour
- 1 tablespoon baking powder
- 1/2 teaspoon baking soda
- 1/2 teaspoon salt
- 1/2 cup cold unsalted butter, cut into small cubes
- 1 cup shredded cheddar cheese (sharp or mild)
- 1/4 cup chopped fresh chives
- 3/4 cup buttermilk (plus extra for brushing)
- 1 large egg, lightly beaten (for egg wash)

Instructions:

1. Preheat Oven and Prepare Baking Sheet:
    - Preheat your oven to 400°F (200°C). Line a baking sheet with parchment paper or a silicone baking mat.
2. Mix Dry Ingredients:
    - In a large bowl, whisk together the flour, baking powder, baking soda, and salt.
3. Cut in Butter:
    - Add the cold butter cubes to the dry ingredients. Using a pastry cutter or your fingers, work the butter into the flour mixture until it resembles coarse crumbs.
4. Add Cheese and Chives:
    - Stir in the shredded cheddar cheese and chopped fresh chives until evenly distributed.
5. Form Dough:
    - Make a well in the center of the mixture and pour in the buttermilk. Stir gently with a wooden spoon or rubber spatula until the dough just comes together. Be careful not to overmix.
6. Shape and Cut Scones:
    - Turn the dough out onto a lightly floured surface. Pat the dough into a circle or rectangle about 1 inch thick.
    - Using a sharp knife or a biscuit cutter, cut the dough into scones of desired shape and size. For traditional triangular scones, cut the circle of dough into 8 wedges.
7. Brush with Egg Wash:
    - Place the scones on the prepared baking sheet. Brush the tops of the scones with the beaten egg wash, which will give them a golden brown color when baked.
8. Bake:
    - Bake in the preheated oven for 15-18 minutes, or until the scones are golden brown on top and cooked through. The bottoms should also be golden brown.
9. Cool and Serve:

- Transfer the cheese and chive scones to a wire rack to cool slightly before serving. Enjoy warm or at room temperature.

Tips:

- Cheese Variation: Experiment with different types of cheese such as Gouda, Swiss, or a combination of cheeses for different flavors.
- Storage: Store leftover scones in an airtight container at room temperature for up to 2 days. Reheat briefly in the oven or toaster oven before serving.
- Serve with: These scones are delicious on their own or served with butter, cream cheese, or a savory spread.

These cheese and chive scones are flaky, cheesy, and bursting with fresh herb flavor. They are perfect for serving alongside soups, salads, or as a standalone snack. Enjoy the homemade goodness of warm scones straight from your oven!

Cheese and Bacon Dip

Ingredients:

- 8 ounces cream cheese, softened
- 1 cup sour cream
- 1 cup shredded cheddar cheese
- 1 cup shredded mozzarella cheese
- 1/2 cup grated Parmesan cheese
- 1/2 cup cooked bacon, crumbled (about 6 slices)
- 2 green onions, thinly sliced (green parts only)
- 1 teaspoon garlic powder
- 1/2 teaspoon onion powder
- Salt and pepper, to taste
- Optional: Chopped fresh parsley or chives for garnish

Instructions:

1. Preheat Oven:
   - Preheat your oven to 350°F (175°C).
2. Mix Ingredients:
   - In a large mixing bowl, combine softened cream cheese, sour cream, shredded cheddar cheese, shredded mozzarella cheese, grated Parmesan cheese, crumbled bacon, sliced green onions, garlic powder, and onion powder. Season with salt and pepper to taste.
3. Bake the Dip:
   - Transfer the mixture to a baking dish or oven-safe skillet, spreading it out evenly.
4. Bake in the Oven:
   - Bake in the preheated oven for 20-25 minutes, or until the cheese is melted and the dip is bubbly and heated through.
5. Garnish and Serve:
   - Remove from the oven and garnish with chopped fresh parsley or chives if desired.
   - Serve the cheese and bacon dip warm with tortilla chips, crackers, bread slices, or fresh vegetables for dipping.

Tips:

- Variations: Add diced jalapeños for a spicy kick, or substitute different types of cheese like Pepper Jack or Gouda for varied flavors.
- Make-Ahead: Prepare the dip up to a day in advance and store it covered in the refrigerator. Bake just before serving.
- Presentation: Serve the dip directly in the baking dish or skillet for a rustic and inviting presentation.

This cheese and bacon dip is creamy, cheesy, and loaded with savory bacon flavor. It's sure to be a crowd-pleaser at your next gathering, providing a deliciously indulgent appetizer that everyone will enjoy dipping into!

Cheese-Stuffed Chicken Parmesan

Ingredients:

- 4 boneless, skinless chicken breasts
- Salt and pepper, to taste
- 1 cup shredded mozzarella cheese
- 1/2 cup grated Parmesan cheese
- 1 cup Italian-style breadcrumbs
- 1/2 cup all-purpose flour
- 2 large eggs, beaten
- 2 cups marinara sauce
- 2 tablespoons olive oil
- Fresh basil leaves, chopped (for garnish)

Instructions:

1. Preheat Oven:
    - Preheat your oven to 375°F (190°C). Lightly grease a baking dish with olive oil or non-stick cooking spray.
2. Prepare Chicken Breasts:
    - Butterfly each chicken breast by slicing horizontally through the center, but not all the way through, to create a pocket. Season both sides of each chicken breast with salt and pepper.
3. Stuff Chicken with Cheese:
    - Stuff each chicken breast with shredded mozzarella cheese. Optionally, you can add sliced or shredded Parmesan cheese as well.
4. Coat Chicken:
    - Set up three shallow dishes: one with flour, one with beaten eggs, and one with breadcrumbs mixed with grated Parmesan cheese. Coat each stuffed chicken breast first in flour, then dip into the beaten eggs, and finally coat with the breadcrumb mixture, pressing gently to adhere.
5. Brown Chicken:
    - Heat olive oil in a large skillet over medium-high heat. Brown the breaded chicken breasts on both sides until golden brown, about 3-4 minutes per side. This step helps to seal in the cheese and adds flavor.
6. Assemble in Baking Dish:
    - Transfer the browned chicken breasts to the prepared baking dish. Spoon marinara sauce over each chicken breast, covering them generously. Top each chicken breast with additional shredded mozzarella cheese.
7. Bake:
    - Bake in the preheated oven for 20-25 minutes, or until the chicken is cooked through (internal temperature of 165°F/75°C) and the cheese is melted and bubbly.

8. Serve:
    - Remove from the oven and let the chicken rest for a few minutes before serving. Garnish with chopped fresh basil leaves if desired.

Tips:

- Cheese Variations: Experiment with different cheeses such as provolone, Fontina, or ricotta for stuffing the chicken breasts.
- Serving Suggestions: Serve cheese-stuffed chicken Parmesan with pasta, garlic bread, or a side salad for a complete meal.
- Make-Ahead: Prepare the chicken breasts up to the browning stage, then refrigerate them covered until ready to bake. Add marinara sauce and cheese just before baking.

This cheese-stuffed chicken Parmesan recipe is sure to impress with its cheesy filling and delicious marinara sauce. It's perfect for a special dinner or when you want to treat yourself to a comforting and satisfying meal!